Canadian Daily Language Activities

—— Grade 2 ——

Written by Eleanor M. Summers

Our Canadian Daily Language Activities series provides short and quick opportunities for students to review and reinforce skills in punctuation, grammar, spelling, language and reading comprehension. The Bonus Activities that follow each week of skills are fun tasks such as word and vocabulary puzzles, figurative language and reading exercises. A short interesting fact about Canada is the finishing touch!

ELEANOR M. SUMMERS is a retired teacher who is still actively involved in education. She has created many resources in language, science and history. As a writer, she enjoys creating practical and thought-provoking resources for teachers and parents.

Published in Canada by:
On The Mark Press
Belleville, ON
www.onthemarkpress.com

Funded by the
Government
of Canada

Canada

#OTM2161

Topics cover:
Small Crawling and Flying Animals; and Animal Growth and Changes.

#OTM2153

Topics cover:
Cover and Topics Covered: Air, Water & Soil in the Environment

15 unit tests include: place value, adding & subtracting numbers to 18 and 2 digit numbers, multiplication, division, money, fractions, data management, probability, patterning, expressions & equality, 2 and 3D geometry, time & temperature and measurement.

#K151

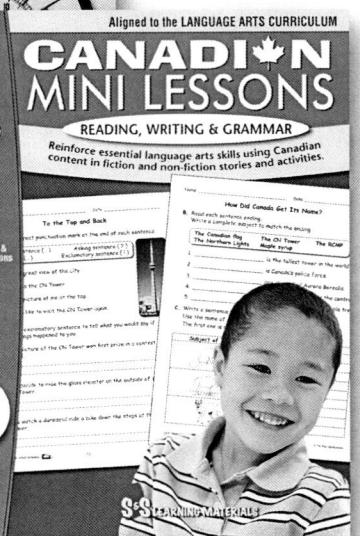

#J182

This resource uses Canadian content for all stories and activities in a variety of genres: fiction, non-fiction, poems. Grammar and writing activities practice and reinforce vocabulary development, spelling, grammar, punctuation and creative writing.

SSR1145   ISBN: 9781771587310 © On The Mark Press

HOW TO USE CANADIAN DAILY LANGUAGE ACTIVITIES

This book is divided into 32 weekly sections.

Each weekly section provides daily skill review and assessment activities.

ACTIVITIES 1 – 4:

Focus is on:

- punctuation, capitalization, grammar and spelling
- language and reading comprehension skills

ACTIVITY 5:

Focus is on:

- a single language or reading skill

BONUS ACTIVITY:

Provides opportunities for extended activities

- word puzzles, vocabulary development
- spelling
- reading skills
- includes a short, interesting fact about Canada

STUDENT PROGRESS CHART

- Students record their daily score for each Language Activity.
- At the end of the week, they calculate their Total Score
- At the end of four weeks, students evaluate their performance.
- Students will require one copy of page 3 and three copies of page 4 to record results for entire 32 weeks. Teachers may wish to make back-to-back copies.

TEACHER SUGGESTIONS

- All activities may be completed for each week or teachers may exclude some.
- New skills may be completed as a whole class activity.
- Bonus Activities may be used at teachers' discretion.
- Correcting student work together will help model the correct responses.
- Monitor student mastery of skills from information on the Student Progress Chart.

_____ 'S PROGRESS CHART

How many did you get correct each day? Record your score on the chart.

Week	Activity 1	Activity 2	Activity 3	Activity 4	Activity 5	Total Score
#	/5	/5	/5	/5	/5	/25

Week	Activity 1	Activity 2	Activity 3	Activity 4	Activity 5	Total Score
#	/5	/5	/5	/5	/5	/25

Week	Activity 1	Activity 2	Activity 3	Activity 4	Activity 5	Total Score
#	/5	/5	/5	/5	/5	/25

Week	Activity 1	Activity 2	Activity 3	Activity 4	Activity 5	Total Score
#	/5	/5	/5	/5	/5	/25

My strongest skills are _____

My skills that need improvement are _____

The Bonus Activities I liked best are _____

Week	Activity 1	Activity 2	Activity 3	Activity 4	Activity 5	Total Score
#	/5	/5	/5	/5	/5	/25

Week	Activity 1	Activity 2	Activity 3	Activity 4	Activity 5	Total Score
#	/5	/5	/5	/5	/5	/25

Week	Activity 1	Activity 2	Activity 3	Activity 4	Activity 5	Total Score
#	/5	/5	/5	/5	/5	/25

Week	Activity 1	Activity 2	Activity 3	Activity 4	Activity 5	Total Score
#	/5	/5	/5	/5	/5	/25

My strongest skills are _____

My skills that need improvement are _____

The Bonus Activities I liked best are _____

SSR1145   ISBN: 9781771587310 © On The Mark Press

_____ 'S PROGRESS CHART

Week	Activity 1	Activity 2	Activity 3	Activity 4	Activity 5	Total Score
#	/5	/5	/5	/5	/5	/25

Week	Activity 1	Activity 2	Activity 3	Activity 4	Activity 5	Total Score
#	/5	/5	/5	/5	/5	/25

Week	Activity 1	Activity 2	Activity 3	Activity 4	Activity 5	Total Score
#	/5	/5	/5	/5	/5	/25

Week	Activity 1	Activity 2	Activity 3	Activity 4	Activity 5	Total Score
#	/5	/5	/5	/5	/5	/25

My strongest skills are _____

My skills that need improvement are _____

The Bonus Activities I liked best are _____

Week	Activity 1	Activity 2	Activity 3	Activity 4	Activity 5	Total Score
#	/5	/5	/5	/5	/5	/25

Week	Activity 1	Activity 2	Activity 3	Activity 4	Activity 5	Total Score
#	/5	/5	/5	/5	/5	/25

Week	Activity 1	Activity 2	Activity 3	Activity 4	Activity 5	Total Score
#	/5	/5	/5	/5	/5	/25

Week	Activity 1	Activity 2	Activity 3	Activity 4	Activity 5	Total Score
#	/5	/5	/5	/5	/5	/25

My strongest skills are _____

My skills that need improvement are _____

The Bonus Activities I liked best are _____

SSR1145   ISBN: 9781771587310 © On The Mark Press

DAILY LANGUAGE ACTIVITIES SKILLS LIST

This book provides many opportunities for practice of the following skills:

VOCABULARY AND WORD SKILLS

- word meaning from context
- root words
- vowel sounds/consonant sounds
- spelling
- syllabication
- synonyms/antonyms/homonyms
- contractions
- rhyming
- compound words
- word families

CAPITALIZATION

- beginning of sentences
- proper names/titles of people
- names of places
- titles of books, songs, poems
- names of days, months, holidays
- abbreviations

PUNCTUATION

- punctuation at the end of a sentence
- commas in a series
- commas in dates and addresses
- periods in abbreviations
- quotation marks in speech
- apostrophes in contractions
- apostrophes in possessives
- punctuation in a friendly letter
- run on sentences

GRAMMAR AND WORD USAGE

Parts of speech:

- nouns, pronouns
- common/proper nouns
- singular/plural nouns
- possessive nouns
- adjectives
- verb forms
- adverbs
- double negatives
- correct article/determiner
- subject – verb agreement
- identifying sentences: sentence vs not a sentence
- sentence types

READING COMPREHENSION

- analogies
- categorization
- cause and effect
- fact or opinion
- real or make-believe
- figurative language
- sequencing

REFERENCE SKILLS

- alphabetical order
- dictionary skills

SSR1145   ISBN: 9781771587310 © On The Mark Press

Name: _____

Correct these sentences.

1. dan and david are cousins

_____

2. can you help me fix this

_____

Circle the action words (verbs).

3. run   down   look   tree

4. sad   baseball   jog   cry

Is this sentence a question or a statement?

5. Where is the soccer ball _____

Name: _____

Sentence or not a sentence?

1. Each morning at breakfast _____

2. Look at the Canada goose _____

Correct these sentences.

3. my library book is at school

_____

4. did you see the rainbow in the sky

_____

Circle the word that is spelled correctly.

5. leef   leafe   lefe   leaf

Name: _____

Circle the words that need capital letters.

1. ontario   forest   bear   manitoba

Correct these sentences.

2. wow, i won first prize

_____

3. where are we going for lunch

_____

Write two more words for each of these word families.

4. - ack family _____   _____

5. - ight family _____   _____

- -

Name: _____

Circle the words that rhyme.

1. book   bark   cook   shook   lot

2. wet   jet   got   pet   cat

Correct these sentences.

3. where are youre new shoes

_____

4. we seen a chipmunk in the yard

_____

Circle the 3 words that have the same beginning sound.

5. city   candy   circle   cake   centre

   SSR1145   ISBN: 9781771587310 © On The Mark Press

Name: _____

Put in the end marks for each sentence: ? , ! , or . Write your answer on the line.

1. Do you have a pet _____

2. I have a cat named Duffy _____

3. What a great idea _____

4. Do you want to play baseball with us _____

5. I love to play Lego with my friends _____

Put a star beside the sentences that are questions.

_____

_____

_____

Name: _____

Bonus Activity: Something Fishy!

Find the names of these Canadian fish in the Word Search puzzle.

Circle your answers.

cod	tuna	herring	salmon	haddock	sole	perch	smelt
b	w	c	s	t	p	e	s
c	a	t	u	d	e	t	m
i	o	n	r	m	r	f	e
h	a	d	d	o	c	k	l
a	k	s	p	n	h	i	t
m	p	u	o	q	k	j	g
p	n	s	a	l	m	o	n
g	n	i	r	r	e	h	h

On July 1, 2017, Canada will be 150 years old.
What a lot of candles!   **MY CANADA**

WEEK 2

ACTIVITY 1

TOTAL /5

Correct these sentences.

1. is they going to move away

_____

2. mom and me is going shopping on saturday

_____

Write the number of syllables (word parts) in each word.

3. canoe   _____

4. summertime   _____

Write the contraction that is made from these two words.

5. I am _____

Name: _____

WEEK 2

ACTIVITY 2

TOTAL /5

Circle Sentence or Not a sentence

1. Back on the shelf.   Sentence   Not a sentence

2. Take the dog for a walk.   Sentence   Not a sentence

Real or make-believe?

3. Canada has four seasons _____

Correct these sentences.

4. the fox live in a den in the field

_____

5. how many fox pups lives with the mother

_____

SSR1145   ISBN: 9781771587310 © On The Mark Press

Name: _____

What do these words have in common?

1. ice cream cone   Popsicle   ice cream sandwich _____

Correct these sentences.

2. lets go catch some fish for dinner

_____

3. we can cook thems in the frying pen

_____

Complete these analogies.

4. Hen is to egg as cow is to _____

5. Girl is to woman as boy is to _____

- -

Name: _____

Correct these sentences.

1. when is harry gettin his new puppy

_____

2. sally and me likes to skip

_____

Write three words in the -ill family

3. _____

Circle the correct meaning for each word.

4. lunch   (a) a new kind of toy   (b) a meal eaten at noon   (c) a special game

5. dance   (a) to sing a song   (b) to play a new game   (c) to move in time to music

Name: _____

Nouns Name Things

A <u>noun</u> is a word that <u>names</u> a person, a place or a thing.

Write the correct word for the noun that matches each picture.

_____	_____	_____	_____	_____

What is true about each word? _____

- -

Name: _____

Bonus Activity: Rhyming Riddles

Read the rhyming clue and the meaning for the new word.

Write your answer and draw a picture to show the word.

Rhyming Clue	Meaning	New Word	My Picture
Rhymes with "dug"	An insect		
Rhymes with "bake"	Something good to eat		
Rhymes with "wish"	It swims in a lake		
Rhymes with "boy"	Something to play with		

*If you have one toonie and two loonies,
how much money do you have?*   ($5.00)   **MY CANADA**

SSR1145   ISBN: 9781771587310 © On The Mark Press

Name: _____

Correct these sentences.

1.   them clowns done funny tricks at the circus

_____

2.   jenny runned fast to wine the race

_____

Write the two words that make each compound word.

3.   sunshine _____

4.   outside _____

Circle the word that comes first in alphabetical order.

5.   ghost   bank   candy   apple   home

- -

Name: _____

Sentence or not a sentence?

1.   A picnic on Sunday._____

2.   We are going to see Grandma._____

Correct these sentences.

3.   my friend, damon, wasnt at school today

_____

4.   i helped uncle jack milk the cows

_____

Circle the abbreviation for "Friday".

5.   Fry.   Frid.   Fri.   Fr.

Name: _____

Circle the word that doesn't belong.

1. four   hockey   eight   three

2. hamster   puppy   cookie   pony

Correct these sentences.

3. tom gived charlie his bestest ball glove

_____

4. when are our class trip to montreal

_____

Real or make-believe?

5. There is a pot of gold at the end of a rainbow. _____

Name: _____

Tell if the underlined word is a <u>noun</u> or a <u>verb</u>.

1. I <u>love</u> chocolate ice cream! _____

2. The mother <u>lion</u> looks after her cubs. _____

Correct these sentences.

3. we is going sailing on the st. lawrence river

_____

4. has the brown family move away yet

_____

Circle the word that is spelled correctly.

5. sale   saile   salle   sile

SSR1145   ISBN: 9781771587310 © On The Mark Press

Name: _____

Nouns name people, places and things.

To make a noun mean more than one, most words add "s".

If the noun ends in "sh", "ch" or "x", add "es"

Make these nouns mean more than one by adding "s" or "es".

1. pencil _____

2. dish _____

3. chair _____

4. fox _____

5. patch _____

Name: _____

Bonus Activity: Giving Thanks

Read the following story about Thanksgiving.

Read the sentences. Circle T if the sentence is TRUE and F if the sentence is FALSE.

Thanksgiving is celebrated on the second Monday in October. It was started many years ago by pioneers. They were thankful for a new life in Canada. Today many families gather for a big Thanksgiving dinner. At my house we have a turkey dinner and pumpkin pie. It is a happy time of the year!

1. T F Thanksgiving is celebrated in November.

2. T F Pioneer families started the first Thanksgiving.

3. T F Today we have a big dinner with our family and friends.

MY CANADA *If the Three Little Pigs moved to Canada's Arctic, where would they live? In a pigaloo!*

Name: _____

Correct these sentences.

1. did her broke that glass dish

_____

2. me and dad went fishin for perch

_____

Number these words in alphabetical order.

3. ..... jam ...... rattle ...... happy ...... summer

Tell how many syllables (word parts) you hear in each word.

4. raccoon _____

5. Vancouver _____

- -

Name: _____

Circle the word that means the same as "little"

1. huge   glad   tiny   slow

Write the two words that make each compound word.

2. baseball _____

3. snowshoe _____

Correct these sentences.

4. mother cat hid her kitens in the barn

_____

5. did your mom made those cookies

_____

SSR1145   ISBN: 9781771587310 © On The Mark Press

Name: _____

Circle the word that does not belong in each group.

1. Thanksgiving   Christmas   Toronto   Easter

2. blue   purple   sunny   green

Correct these sentences.

3. did you learn how to skate last year

_____

4. ill ask my dad if i can go with you

_____

Write two words in the -ing family.

5. - ing _____   _____

- -

Name: _____

Circle the word that is spelled correctly in each group.

1. wiht   wif   with   withe

2. bute   but   bote   botte

Correct these sentences.

3. we seed a lot of mouses in the old shed

_____

4. do you think our cat, sally, can catch them

_____

Circle the correct abbreviation for "November"

5. Novem.   Novemb.   Novmbr.   Nov.

Tell if the sentence is a <u>statement</u> or a <u>question</u>. Put a ? or a . at the end.

1. Do you have a new kitten _____

2. I saw a gorilla at the zoo _____

3. I like the movie called Zootopia _____

4. Have you seen it yet _____

5. Next week I am going to Winnipeg _____

Name: _____

Bonus Activity: Weather Nouns

These words name weather words. Solve the puzzle by filling in the correct word.

cloud   rain   snow   hail   wind

	Clue							
1	You can make a snow-fort with me.							
2	You will get wet when I fall on you.							
3	I am balls of ice that fall to earth.							
4	I can be strong or gentle when I blow.							
5	I can be white and fluffy or very dark.							

The moose population in Newfoundland and Labrador is higher than anywhere else in North America... more than 150, 000 in total!

MY CANADA

SSR1145   ISBN: 9781771587310 © On The Mark Press

Name: _____

One or more than one?

1. children _____

Correct these sentences.

2. did your baby brother take your cookie

    _____

3. i seen a rainbow in the skye today

    _____

Write statement, command, question or exclamation to tell the kind of sentence.

4. Are you a good soccer player _____

5. Hurrah, I won _____

- -

Name: _____

Real or make-believe?

1. You can spin straw into gold. _____
2. Fishermen catch lobsters in traps. _____

Correct these sentences.

3. marty live in langley, british columbia

    _____

4. are you going in the terry fox run

    _____

Make this noun mean more than one.

5. camper _____

Write the correct word on the line.

1. Theo is the _____ runner in our class.

    fast / faster / fastest

2. Today is _____ than yesterday.

    sunny / sunnier / sunniest

Number these words in alphabetical order.

3. ...... bet   ...... bat   ...... but   ...... bit

Correct these sentences.

4. please bee on time for our game on saturday

    _____

5. brang your lunch a water bottle and sunscreen

    _____

Tell how many syllables (word parts) are in this word.

1. Ontario _____

Correct these sentences.

2. were going to nova scotia in august

    _____

3. are you gonna visit your aunt betty

    _____

Complete the analogies

4. bee is to hive as bird is to _____

5. duck is to duckling as hen is to _____

SSR1145   ISBN: 9781771587310 © On The Mark Press

Name: _____

Tricky Nouns

Plural nouns mean more than one person, place or thing.

Nouns that end in "y", change "y" to "i' and add "es".

Some tricky nouns change to a new word.

Write the plural for each of these nouns.

1. baby _____

2. story _____

3. foot _____

4. child _____

5. man _____

Name: _____

Bonus Activity: Homophones

Homophones are words that sound the same but have different meanings and spellings. Read each pair of homophones. Circle the correct word that matches the picture.

deer	pair	eight	pale	toe	won
dear	pear	ate	pail	tow	one

What animal appears on Canada's nickel? A beaver.

MY CANADA

Name: _____

Correct these sentences.

1. terry goed fishin in the pond

    _____

2. did hims catch eny fish to ate

    _____

Circle the correct word to fit in each sentence.

3. I (is, am) going to the Calgary Stampede.

4. We (is, are) going this summer.

Write the two words that make each contraction.

5. don't _____   that's _____

- -

Name: _____

Write three words that rhyme with "few"

1. _____   _____   _____

What is this person probably doing?

2. Jackie swung the bat as hard as he could. _____

3. We climbed to the top, sat down, and slid to the ground. _____

Correct these sentences.

4. our cat runned after the mices

    _____

5. her likes to show me when her catches won

    _____

SSR1145   ISBN: 9781771587310 © On The Mark Press

Name: _____

Write two words in the "oi" family.

1. _____

Circle the verb in each sentence.

2. The children splashed around in the pool.

3. Sammy named his duck Little Peep.

Correct these sentences.

4. has you ever read the book <u>flat stanley</u>

_____

5. how meny sheeps is in the pen

_____

- -

Name: _____

Correct these sentences.

1. dont you has no cookys to share

_____

2. this here game are fun to play

_____

Sentence or not a sentence?

3. Made a birthday cake. _____

4. My sister's birthday is on Sunday. _____

Circle the words that need capitals in this sentence.

5. david is playing soccer for the rosetown runners

Name: _____

Verbs show **action** and tell us **what is happening** in a sentence. Pick a verb from this list to complete each sentence: *roar, help, scores, howl, comes*

1   Can you hear the wolves _____ at night?

2.   I will _____ Mom do the dishes.

3.   Lions _____ to scare their enemies.

4.   Here _____ the Canada Day parade!

5.   Grant _____ the most goals in hockey.

Name: _____

Bonus Activity: Animal Categories

Write these animal names in the correct category.

| lizard | blue jay | tuna | bear | raccoon | salamander |
| loon | snake | beaver | goose | cod | haddock |

Birds	Fish	Mammals	Reptiles

MY CANADA
What animal is furry, has antlers and is very scary? A *cariBOO!*

     SSR1145   ISBN: 9781771587310 © On The Mark Press

Name: _____

Correct these sentences.

1. our dog jake need a bath last night

   _____

2. him were running through mudd puddles

   _____

Circle the misspelled word in each sentence.

3. That was a funney story we read.

4. May I play wiht you and your team?

Real or make-believe?

5. Only boys play hockey. _____

- -

Name: _____

Write the plural form for the following nouns

1. box _____

2. lady _____

Write an antonym for this word.

3. dull _____

Correct these sentences.

4. my litle sister are too years old in april

   _____

5. ms hunt read <u>anne of green gables</u> to our class

   _____

Name: _____

Circle the words that are in the same group.

1. lake   pond   mountain   river   tunnel

Correct these sentences.

2. why is we staying home this here weekend

_____

3. you needs to clean your roome

_____

Write the number of syllables (word parts) in each word.

4. Toronto   _____

5. Rocky Mountains _____

- -

Name: _____

Correct these sentences.

1. andy and luke wasnt at sckool today

_____

2. molly were surprised when her gots a new puppy

_____

Circle the words that are plural.

3. babies   leaves   woman   telephone   feet

Write the possessive form of the noun

4. the hat of my Grandpa _____

5. the friend of Kenny _____

 SSR1145   ISBN: 9781771587310 © On The Mark Press

Name: _____

Contractions in Sentences

Write a contraction for the two words in brackets.

1. _____ (They have) been playing baseball all day.

2. _____ (Who is) going to be on our team?

3. _____ (Are not) you coming with us to the beach?

4. _____ (We are) going to swim and have a picnic.

5. _____ (Let us) invite Roger and Abi to come with us.

- -

Name: _____

Bonus Activity: Crack the Code

Use this code to find out what the sentence is asking. Then answer the question.

1	2	3	4	5	6	7	8	9	10	11	12	13	14	15	16	17	18	19	20	21	22	23	24	25	26
a	b	c	d	e	f	g	h	i	j	k	l	m	n	o	p	q	r	s	t	u	v	w	x	y	z

23	8	1	20		3	15	12	15	21	18		9	19		15	21	18		6	12	1	7	
																						?	

My answer is _____

The Hotel de Glace in Quebec is rebuilt every winter because it melts in summer.

MY CANADA

Name: _____

Correct these sentences.

1. thats the smallest kitten i ever seen

_____

2. allan went to sea dr hardy

_____

Write the two words that make up each compound word.

3. fireplace _____

4. sailboat _____

Circle the one that is correct.

5.   Hamilton Ontario,   Hamilton, Ontario   Hamilton, Ontario,

- -

Name: _____

Circle the verbs in each sentence.

1.   Bobby ran down the lane and jumped over the fence.

2.   Callie cried when she lost her jacket.

Circle the word that is spelled correctly.

3.   whit   whiet   white   wite

Correct these sentences.

4.   ill help you cleen your room todaye

_____

5.   whats youre favourite snack four school

_____

SSR1145   ISBN: 9781771587310 © On The Mark Press

Name: _____

Write a common noun for each proper noun.

1. Montreal   _____

2. Toronto Blue Jays _____

Correct these sentences.

3. can you sing the song "rain, rain, go away"

_____

4. my favourite foods are pizza milk and ice cream

_____

Is this sentence a statement, question, command or exclamation?

5. Close the gate and lock it. _____

Name: _____

Correct these sentences.

1. jeffs dad taked the car to wash it

_____

2. we needs to hurry or well miss the bus

_____

Write the word that best completes the sentence.

3. _____ the best chocolate cake in the world!
    Thats / Thats' / That's

Write the compound word made from these words.

4. tooth + brush = _____

5. rain + coat = _____

Combine these sentences to make one good sentence.

1. I like ice cream. Chocolate is my favourite.

    _____

2. Those puppies are cute. They are black lab pups.

    _____

3. My birthday is on Saturday. I am having a party.

    _____

4. We played a game of ball. We played in the backyard.

    _____

5. Aunt Jane is coming tomorrow. She is coming from Moncton.

    _____

Bonus Activity: Colour Unscramble

Unscramble the letters to spell a colour. Write your answer beside the *. Colour the box the colour that matches your word.

lyewol	enreg	perplu	uble	geraon	norwb
*	*	*	*	*	*

What colour is a Canadian ten-dollar bill? Purple.

MY CANADA

   SSR1145   ISBN: 9781771587310 © On The Mark Press

Name: _____

Write a word that is opposite of each word.

1. sunny _____

2. strong _____

Correct these sentences.

3. was you following that pathe through the woods

_____

4. there werent no cookys in the jar

_____

Circle the words that have the sound of "c" in "cent"

5. city   cattle   cereal   cold   circle

Name: _____

Circle the words that mean more than one.

1. cherrys   cherry   cherries

2. man   men   mans

Real or make-believe?

3. Penguins live in Canada's Arctic. _____

Correct these sentences.

4. there is for blue eggs in that there nest

_____

5. when will them eggs hatch

_____

Name: _____

Circle the subject of this sentence.

1.   Harriet and her sister want a goldfish for a pet.

Correct these sentences.

2.   did all them apples fall frum that tree

_____

3.   dad taked us to niagara falls

_____

How many syllables (word parts) does each word have?

4.   Wonderland   _____

5.   ferris wheel   _____

- -

Name: _____

Correct these sentences.

1.   josh losted too tooths this week

_____

2.   do you live in alberta ontario or quebec

_____

Use context clues to explain the meaning of the underlined word in this sentence.

3.   We found an old <u>trunk</u> in the attic.

_____

Where would each event probably take place?

4.   We played games and had cake and ice cream. _____

5.   Kelly built a big sand castle. _____

SSR1145   ISBN: 9781771587310 © On The Mark Press

Rewrite this letter. Correct the mistakes.

Deer Logan

   can you come to my house on friday night

You and me will have fun playing Lego

bye for now

reese

_____

_____

_____

_____

Bonus Activity: Double, Double

Complete each sentence with a word from the Word Box.

manners	summer	bubble	paddle	fluffy

1. I love to chew _____ gum!

2. Those clouds are white and _____.

3. My favourite season is _____

4. Dad lets me _____ our canoe.

5. I like people with good _____

Why is it so cold in a hockey rink? There are lots of fans!

MY CANADA

Write two words for each of these word families.

1. - ate _____

2. - ue _____

Correct these sentences.

3. why was the boys running away from you

_____

4. toby singed a song all by hisself

_____

Complete the analogy.

5. King is to prince as queen is to _____

Circle the verb in each sentence.

1. Gary laughed at the funny clown.

2. The wind blew hard all night long.

Circle the word that doesn't belong.

3. coat   hat   mittens   boys   scarf

Correct these sentences.

4. has you read the story goodnight, mr moon

_____

5. we doesnt go to school in july or august

_____

SSR1145 ISBN: 9781771587310 © On The Mark Press

Name: _____

Number these words in alphabetical order.

1. ...... bear   ...... bite   ...... bake   ...... bottle

Correct these sentences.

2. how big is wally's new soccer shoes

_____

3. it might rein so takes youre umbrella

_____

Circle the nouns in each sentence.

4. The clown had a big red nose.

5. Are the boys running in this race?

- -

Name: _____

Correct these sentences.

1. werent that the funniest story you ever heared

_____

2. didnt you bring them there treats for us

_____

Write two words that rhyme with this word

3. shakes _____

Write a pronoun to replace the underlined word.

4. <u>Mary</u> rode her bike home. _____

5. We laughed at <u>the joke</u>. _____

Combine these sentences into one good sentence.

1. A plane flew over my house. It was a big plane.

    _____

2. We are having hot dogs tonight. We are having hamburgers too.

    _____

3. Did Harry go swimming? Did he go swimming in the lake?

    _____

4. I have homework to do. It is math homework.

    _____

5. A bird is in the birdbath. It is a robin.

    _____

Bonus Activity: Words with - igh

Find and circle these words in the Word Search puzzle.

sigh   night   highway   right   fight   high   mighty   sight

h	g	i	h	p	e	f	z
s	i	g	h	g	w	h	t
t	h	g	i	f	v	e	h
a	n	t	h	g	i	r	g
f	s	i	l	w	b	k	i
c	e	e	g	r	a	l	s
f	m	i	g	h	t	y	x
h	s	k	o	q	t	q	c

Canada has about 140,000 different species of animals.

MY CANADA

Name: _____

Correct these sentences.

1. i has a samwich and too cookies in my lunch

_____

2. does you like chocklit milk or white milk

_____

Write 3 words to rhyme with each word below.

3. cry _____   _____   _____

4. flew. _____   _____   _____

Write the word that is missing.

5. We are _____ to the beach.

    gone / went / going

- -

Name: _____

Write <u>sentence</u> or not a <u>sentence</u>.

1. Snowed all day_____

2. We built a snowfort in the yard_____

Correct these sentences.

3. aunt darlene cooked a turkey for sunday dinner

_____

4. mark and i eated a big drumstick all bye ourselves

_____

Write the number of syllables in

5. bicycle _____

Name: _____

Correct these sentences.

1. me and sonya was laughing at the funny show

_____

2. it were about a talkin cow named daisy

_____

Circle the subject of the sentence.

3. Amy loves to draw and colour.

4. Cheese is a healthy snack.

Write the correct word on the line.

5. George is the _____ boy in my class.   tall   taller   tallest

_____

- -

Name: _____

Real or make-believe?

1. The sky can look red in a sunset. _____

2. Some beans can grow a giant beanstalk. _____

Correct these sentences.

3. dont put them dirty shoes on the cleen flore

_____

4. why doesn't you wippe thems off outside

_____

Circle the words that are verbs.

5. We shouted and cheered for the home team.

SSR1145   ISBN: 9781771587310 © On The Mark Press

Name: _____

Write the word or words that best complete each sentence.

1. I am _____ to build a farm with my Lego.
   went / going / gone

2. Of all my toys, I like Lego the _____.
   good / better / best

3. Sometimes I _____ and play with it for hours.
   set / sit / sat

4. I _____ there is a new set with animals.
   herd / heard / heared

5. I am going to ask my mom to _____ that set for my birthday.
   bought / buying / buy

- -

Name: _____

Bonus Activity: Action Word Puzzle

Write a word from the Word Box to match the clue.

Word Box: climb   draw   laugh   read   run   sing

Word Clues: You do this					
1. if you are in a race.					
2. with a song.					
3. with a book.					
4. to make a picture.					
5. to get to the top of a hill.					
6. when something is funny.					

On which Canadian coin would you find a polar bear? Toonie.   **MY CANADA**

Name: _____

Explain the meaning of the underlined words.

1.   Jack was <u>as hungry as a bear</u>. _____

Correct these sentences.

2.   annie's birthday is on monday august 21

_____

3.   is you gonna go to hers birthday party

_____

Write the correct pronoun to replace the underlined noun.

4.   <u>Sammy and Sue</u> have a new pug puppy. _____

5.   <u>Their puppy</u> follows them everywhere. _____

Name: _____

Correct these sentences.

1.   them socks is too small for my feat

_____

2.   does you have a pear i could borrow

_____

Circle the word that is spelled correctly in each row.

3.   runing   talkking   laughing   smileing

4.   drinck   drenck   dreank   drink

Write two words that rhyme with "boat"

5.   _____   _____

        SSR1145   ISBN: 9781771587310 © On The Mark Press

Correct these sentences.

1.   me and my sister likes to play in the sand

_____

2.   we builded a hug sand castle with too towers

_____

Circle the whole predicate in each sentence.

3.   We skated for three hours on the pond.

4.   We drank hot chocolate to warm up.

Common noun or proper noun?

5.   Toronto Raptors _____

- -

Correct these sentences.

1.   dont step in that there puddle

_____

2.   isnt you wearing your knew shoes

_____

Write the two words used to make each contraction.

3.   don't _____

4.   I'm _____

Number these words in alphabetical order.

5.   ..... belt   ..... bolt   ..... baby   .... burn

Write the correct word on the line.

1. They _____ going to the circus on Saturday.
    is / are

2. Logan _____ know the answer to that question.
    can't / doesn't

3. Mom _____ spaghetti for supper last night.
    made /make

4. Our class _____ singing a song at the concert.
    are / is

5. We _____ want to stay home from the movie.
    isn't /don't

Bonus Activity: The Long and Short of It

Read the words in the boxes.

If the vowel sound in the word is <u>short</u>, colour the box <u>yellow.</u>

If the vowel sound in the word is <u>long</u>, colour the box <u>green.</u>

pen	mice	tub	cane
came	rat	jet	rule
mule	nine	cake	top

What kind of ball cannot bounce? *A snowball!*

MY CANADA

SSR1145   ISBN: 9781771587310 © On The Mark Press

Name: _____

Circle the word that is the opposite of "run".

1. sleep   talk   work   walk   sing

Correct these sentences.

2. does you like apples oranges and grapes

   _____

3. them boys didnt do nothing bad

   _____

Write two compound words that use these words: *some snow where man*

4. _____

5. _____

Name: _____

Write an antonym for each word.

1. sick _____

2. near _____

Correct these sentences.

3. do jenny lives on main street

   _____

4. yes, her live at 205 main street

   _____

Write the missing word on the line.   *goose   gooses   geese*

5. A flock of Canada _____ flew high in the sky.

Name: _____

Circle the correct meaning for the underlined word.

1. Molly has a new pair of shoes.
   (a) a fruit
   (b) two of something

Correct these sentences.

2. has you heared the song called <u>twinkle, twinkle, little star</u>

_____

3. meny childrens nose that there song

_____

Write two words from the "own" family

4. _____

5. _____

- -

Name: _____

Put the quotation marks in the right place in this sentence.

1. What would you like for lunch? asked Tom.

Correct these sentences.

2. willy am takeing hims dog, barney, for a walk

_____

3. barney like to role in the grass and the mudd

_____

Write the root word for each word.

4. bringing _____

5. getting _____

SSR1145 ISBN: 9781771587310 © On The Mark Press

Read the sentences below. Number them in the correct order to tell a story.

_____ We are all packed for the trip.

_____ Mom and Dad said I could ask a friend to go.

_____ We are going on a short vacation.

_____ I am taking my pal, Shelby.

_____ I am really excited to be going.

- -

Name: _____

Bonus Activity: Odd Word Out

Read the words in each box. Draw a line through the word that doesn't belong.

bacon	eggs	toast	pencil	milk
soccer	basketball	baseball	swimming	sweater
pencil	eraser	ruler	hammer	paper
shoes	coat	truck	mittens	hat
cows	books	chickens	horses	pigs

There are over 12,500 shoes and related
MY CANADA   objects in the Bata Shoe Museum in Toronto.

Name: _____

Correct these sentences.

1. ben didnt no the way to kelly's house

   _____

2. the hens on Grandpas farm lay lottsa eggs

   _____

How many syllables in this word?

3. Edmonton _____

Write a common noun for each proper noun.

4. Vancouver Canucks _____

5. St. Lawrence _____

Name: _____

Correct these sentences.

1. the bestest day of the year is july 1 2017

   _____

2. thats the day canada will be 150 yeers old

   _____

Give two words that rhyme with each of these words.

3. grow _____   _____

4. bright _____   _____

What do these words have in common?

5. skis   snowshoes   snowboard   sled _____

SSR1145   ISBN: 9781771587310 © On The Mark Press

Write the two words that make up each contraction.

1. should've _____ _____

2. I'll _____ _____

Correct these sentences.

3. them bees was buzing around the flowers in hims garden

_____

4. him grows vegetables like carots, beens, and korn

_____

Tell if these words are synonyms or antonyms

5. dry   damp _____

- -

Correct these sentences.

1. will you help me built a snofort in mine yard

_____

2. it will makes a good clubhouse for hour frends

_____

Write the pronoun that would replace the underlined words.

3. Dad is making me a car for the soapbox derby. _____

4. My car will be red with orange and yellow flames. _____

What is the meaning of the underlined word.

5. The dog guards the flock of sheep to keep them safe. _____

Rewrite this letter correctly.

February 10 2017

dear ella

   family day is coming soon my mom says i can invite you over to our house she will take us to pizza hut let me know if you can come

your friend

chloe

_____

_____

_____

_____

- -

Bonus Activity: We Get Around

Write these ways of transportation in the correct category.

cat	canoe	jet ski	helicopter	van	train
jet	kayak	submarine	hot air balloon	drone	bicycle

Land	Air	Water

Do you like cheese and macaroni?

MY CANADA

Canadians buy this food more than any other in the store.

SSR1145   ISBN: 9781771587310 © On The Mark Press

Name: _____

Write the word that is missing on the line.

1. I think Canada is the _____ country in the world!

   good / better / best

2. Which province is the _____ ?

   big / bigger / biggest

Circle the correct abbreviation for January.

3. Janu.   Janry.   Jan.   Janar.

Correct these sentences.

4. can you gets to cookys for me pleese

   _____

5. i wood also likes a glass of milke

   _____

- -

Name: _____

Write sentence or not a sentence.

1. Too much ice cream last night. _____

Correct these sentences.

2. there is for childrens in my family

   _____

3. i has won sister and too bothers

   _____

Write the plural form of the following nouns.

4. mouse   _____

5. bench   _____

Name: _____

How many syllables in this word?

1. Dawson City _____

Circle the verbs in each sentence.

2. Max picked up the bat, hit the ball and ran to first base.

3. Gabby danced and sang in the show and bowed at the end.

Correct these sentences.

4. him eight a big piece of chockolit cake

_____

5. mine mom maid pan cakes for beekfast this here morning

_____

Name: _____

Circle the subjects in these sentences.

1. The squirrels and chipmunks are gathering nuts.

2. Alex and Andy are running a race.

Correct these sentences.

3. do your aunt wanda live in saskatoon

_____

4. she come to visit yore family each july, dont her

_____

Write two words that rhyme with the following word.

5. dice _____ _____

SSR1145   ISBN: 9781771587310 © On The Mark Press

Yum! Yum!

Number these sentences in order to tell how to make Cinnamon Toast.

_____ Eat and enjoy!

_____ Put the slices of bread into the toaster.

_____ Sprinkle some brown sugar and cinnamon on the buttered toast.

_____ Butter the toasted bread.

_____ Take out two slices of bread.

WEEK
15

ACTIVITY
5

TOTAL
/5

Bonus Activity: Canada's Countryside

Find and circle these words in the Word Search puzzle.

stream   rocks   hills   animals   bugs   flowers   grass   ponds   birds

s	k	c	o	r	w	b	u	g	s
f	t	w	q	w	f	i	r	j	d
l	g	r	a	s	s	r	d	k	o
o	a	g	e	k	a	d	p	q	o
w	f	o	z	a	v	s	o	s	w
e	g	s	l	a	m	i	n	a	h
r	u	p	c	m	b	i	d	b	r
s	l	l	i	h	y	l	s	c	u

WEEK
15

BONUS!
ACTIVITY

What do toads build to honour themselves? Toadem poles!

MY CANADA

WEEK
16

ACTIVITY
1

TOTAL
/5

Where would this event likely happen?

1.   We opened our books and began to read. _____

Circle the adjectives in these sentences.

2.   Mom bought new red shoes.

3.   That little, spotted puppy is named Woof.

Correct these sentences.

4.   why didnt you come over too play last night

_____

5.   we played soccer basketball and tag

_____

- -

Name: _____

WEEK
16

ACTIVITY
2

TOTAL
/5

Real or make-believe?

1.   Dinosaurs roamed the province of Alberta. _____

Write two words that rhyme with each of the following words.

3.   inner _____   _____

3.   dash _____   _____

Correct these sentences.

4.   my cousen and me seen a octopus at marine marvels

_____

5.   it have ate long arms and squirks blew ink

_____

SSR1145   ISBN: 9781771587310 © On The Mark Press

Name: _____

Write the quotation marks in the correct place.

1. Let's play Hide and Seek, said Eddie.

2. Okay. You're It, replied Paula

Tell the kind of sentence: telling, asking, or exclamation.

3. Wow! What a great bike! _____

Correct these sentences.

4. did you brush your tooths and comb your hare

_____

5. the techer like my story called the shy dragon

_____

- -

Name: _____

Correct these sentences.

1. does her like to watch a movie with you

_____

2. did the babys toy fell on the floor

_____

Tell if these nouns are common or proper.

3. Superman _____

4. wagons _____

Write the singular form of this noun.

5. wolves _____

Name: _____

Read the following story. Complete the sentences using words from the story.

Our sun is a star that makes its own light. It is at the centre of our solar system. Earth travels around the sun. When the sun shines, it gives off heat and keeps us warm. The sun makes plants grow. We need the sun to help us grow food.

1. Our sun makes its own _____.

2. When the sun shines, it gives off _____.

3. This heat keeps us _____.

4. Plants need the sun to help them _____.

5. The sun helps us to grow _____.

Name: _____

Bonus Activity: A New Playground

Pretend you are planning a new playground. Read each sentence. Then draw and colour the objects named.

1. Draw a ground line for your plan. Colour the sky <u>blue</u> and the grass <u>green</u>.

2. Draw and colour <u>three trees</u> on each side of your plan.

3. Draw some swings and a slide near one group of trees.

About 30% of Canada's population speaks French. **MY CANADA**

 SSR1145   ISBN: 9781771587310 © On The Mark Press

Name: _____

Correct these sentences.

1.   does you wants to go swimming with use

_____

2.   dont leave them toys on the stares

_____

Write the root word for these words.

3.   dresses   _____

4.   slammed   _____

Circle the words that have the same sound as "ea" in "bread"

5.   each   head   spread   reach   ahead

- -

Name: _____

Circle the words that name people.

1.   dentist   beagle   James   nurse   parrot

Correct these sentences.

2.   they is comeing to our hose to visit on thursday

_____

3.   did that there bear eat sum berrys from the bush

_____

Where does the apostrophe go?

4.   Peters marbles

5.   The farmers horse

Name: _____

Tell the part of speech of the underlined word.

1. The <u>weather</u> is warm today. _____

2. Sometimes it <u>rains</u> for days. _____

Circle the word that is spelled correctly.

3. camara   camira   camera   cemera

Correct these sentences.

4. what would you lick for yore birthday presant

_____

5. there was a lot of mouses in Grandpas barn

_____

Name: _____

Real or make-believe?

1. Icebergs can be seen in the Atlantic Ocean. _____

2. Lions roam wild in Alberta. _____

Correct these sentences.

3. we loves to here the story <u>charlotte's web</u>

_____

4. fern owns a pig named wilbur who meats charlotte

_____

Write an synonym for each word.

5. huge _____   small _____

SSR1145   ISBN: 9781771587310 © On The Mark Press

Name: _____

Cause and Effect

Draw a line to match each cause with its effect.

17

ACTIVITY
5

1. If you fall into the pond   * it will die.

2. If you sleep in   * you will get wet.

3. If you don't water the plant   * you will get them all right.

4. If you join our game   * you might be late for school.

5. If you study your spelling words   * you will have fun.

TOTAL
/5

Name: _____

Bonus Activity: Arctic Animals

WEEK
17

Use this code to spell the names of these Arctic animals.

1	2	3	4	5	6	7	8	9	10	11	12	13	14	15	16	17	18	19	20	21	22	23	24	25	26
a	b	c	d	e	f	g	h	i	j	k	l	m	n	o	p	q	r	s	t	u	v	w	x	y	z

BONUS ACTIVITY

1. ___ ___ ___ ___
   19   5   1   12

2. ___ ___ ___ ___
   23   15   12   6

3. ___ ___ ___ ___ ___ ___ ___
   3   1   18   9   2   15   15

4. ___ ___ ___ ___ ___ ___ ___ ___ ___
   16   15   12   1   18   2   5   1   18

5. ___ ___ ___ ___ ___ ___ ___ ___ ___
   1   18   3   20   9   3   6   15   24

What animal might you see walking along a highway in Newfoundland? A moose.

MY CANADA

SSR1145   ISBN: 9781771587310 © On The Mark Press   57

Name: _____

Write the correct word on the line.

1. Dad has _____ our car to the garage.   took / taking / taken

2. My sister will be _____ in the Ice Show.   skated / skating / skate

Correct these sentences.

3. the browns is moveing to winnipeg

_____

4. i well miss my frends, brandon and kent

_____

Circle the compound words..

5. At our winter carnival, we made snowmen, a snowfort and giant snowballs.

Name: _____

Write the meaning of the underlined expression.

1. It was raining <u>cats and dogs</u>. _____

2. He was walking along <u>like a snail</u>. _____

Correct these sentences.

3. well you fead the dog asked mom

_____

4. dont ferget to give it water she added

_____

Write sentence or not a sentence.

5. The day of the party arrived at last. _____

   SSR1145   ISBN: 9781771587310 © On The Mark Press

Name: _____

Correct these sentences.

1. katie said them girls likes to ride horses

_____

2. which gerl races and jumps i asked

_____

Tell how many syllables in each word.

3. Montreal _____

4. Sudbury _____

Circle the words that rhyme.

5. bee   bed   three   sea   dread   key

- -

Name: _____

Number these words in alphabetical order.

1. ..... hand   ..... habit   ..... hall   ..... hard   ..... hair

Correct these sentences.

2. mother robin pelled a long werm frum the ground

_____

3. she flyed to her next to feed her babys

_____

Where would these events likely take place?

4. "Would you like a menu?" asked the waitress. _____

5. "On your mark. Get set. Go!" _____

Name: _____

Write one of these words on the line to make the sentence correct: *is, are, am*

1. I _____ going to the zoo.

2. Parkwood Zoo _____ very large.

3. There _____ many wild animals to see.

4. The hippos and the giraffes _____ next to each other.

5. I _____ going to work at a zoo some day.

Name: _____

Bonus Activity: Adverbs

Adverbs tell when, where or how an action happens or takes place. Circle each adverb in the sentences below.

1. My brother and I plant seeds indoors in March.

2. The plants grow slowly at first.

3. Later, we plant the tiny plants outdoors.

4. The warm sun makes them grow quickly.

5. Soon there are plants everywhere!

What is a Canadian hairdresser's favourite sport? Curling!

MY CANADA

SSR1145   ISBN: 9781771587310 © On The Mark Press

Name: _____

Correct these sentences.

1. garth say him want a hamster fore a pet

_____

2. him think they are funy litle animals

_____

What is this person probably doing?

3. We need to pack our swimsuits, towels and some lunch.

_____

Give an antonym for each word.

4. tall _____

5. cloudy _____

- -

Name: _____

Circle the words that have the same sound as "aw" in "saw"

1. draw   but   cause   boy   raw   auto

Correct these sentences.

2. mom say vegetables is good for you to eet

_____

3. i likes corn carots peas and potatos

_____

Circle the words that go together.

4. nickle   dime   forest   quarter   trees

5. oranges   grass   apples   pond   peaches

Name: _____

Circle the words that tell about a grizzly bear.

WEEK
19

ACTIVIT
3

TOTAL
/5

1.   furry   blue   strong   hunts   slow

Underline the subject and circle the predicate in each sentence.

2.   The sun shone on the water.

3.   The mother sang a song to her baby.

Correct these sentences.

4.   well you came to my hose to play on saturday

_____

5.   lets build a play ferm with animals and burns

_____

- -

Name: _____

Who might be saying the following?

WEEK
19

ACTIVIT
4

TOTAL
/5

1.   "Remember, practice is after school tonight." _____

2.   "This glass slipper fits just right."_____

Circle the word that is spelled correctly.

3.   isnt   is'nt   i'snt   isn't   isnt'

Correct these sentences.

4.   which story does you like the bestest, <u>gone</u> or <u>happy harry</u>

_____

5.   i likes <u>gone</u> becuz it are a misstery story

_____

     SSR1145   ISBN: 9781771587310 © On The Mark Press

Name: _____

Read the sentences below. Circle the words that need capital letters.

1. carter has to go to the dentist on tuesday.

2. his dentist, dr. ashton, is very nice.

3. her office is on bank street in ottawa.

4. carter is going with his aunt carrie.

5. maybe they will go to pizza hut for lunch

- -

Name: _____

Bonus Activity: On the Farm I Hear .....

Read the words in the box. Write the sound that matches each animal in the speech bubble.

| neigh neigh | oink oink | cluck cluck | moo moo | quack quack | baa baa |

*About 60% of the **world's polar bears** live in Canada.*

MY CANADA

Name: _____

Complete the analogy.

1. Bee is to hive as bird is to _____

Write the two words that make each compound word.

2. cupcake _____

3. lighthouse _____

Correct these sentences.

4. well you helps me with this here homewerk

_____

5. miss melrose sayed we need to finnish it for friday

_____

Name: _____

Correct these sentences.

1. we is gonna go skateing at the woodstock arena

_____

2. lets meat there at 700 on thursday night

_____

How many syllables in each word?

3. toboggan _____

4. snowshoe _____

Write a proper noun for the common noun.

5. hockey team _____

SSR1145   ISBN: 9781771587310 © On The Mark Press

Write the correct abbreviation for:

1.   Thursday _____

Correct these sentences.

2.   my babby sister, amy, crys when her is hungry

_____

3.   my mom feds her and rock her to sleep

_____

Write the two words used to make each contraction.

4.   won't _____

5.   they'll _____

- -

Write the root word for each of these words.

1.   careless   _____

2.   untie   _____

Correct these sentences.

3.   mr and mrs lee is goin away to halifax

_____

4.   they is leavin at 800 on friday mornin

_____

Circle the words that do not belong.

5.   hammer   apples   nails   saw   cucumbers

We add 's (apostrophe + s) to the end of a word to tell that something belongs to someone.

Put the apostrophe in the correct place in the underlined words.

Write the correct form on the line.

1. Carols hair is curly but Annas hair is straight. _____

2. That girls dress is very fancy. _____

3. Jacobs wagon has a broken wheel. _____

4. Dannys new winter coat is red and black. _____

5. My brothers dream is to be a baseball player. _____

- -

Name: _____

Bonus Activity: You, the Artist

BONUS!
ACTIVITY

Read the story. Illustrate each sentence in the box above it.

It was Janie's 8th birthday.	She was going to the park with her friends.	They played on the swings and slides.	Janie had a birthday cake with yellow icing.

"Beaver tails" are a delicious pastry made in Canada.

MY CANADA

SSR1145   ISBN: 9781771587310 © On The Mark Press

Name: _____

Tell what kind of sentence: statement, question, or exclamation.

1. Where are we going for lunch _____

2. Today is Eddie's birthday _____

Correct these sentences.

3. gayle are the short girl in our whole class

_____

4. mine toys is all in that there blew box

_____

Write the root word for:

5. happiness _____

Name: _____

Correct these sentences.

1. mr larson am are next dore neighbour

_____

2. him work with my dad in cranbrook

_____

Give two words that rhyme with each of these words.

3. dark _____

4. came _____

Tell where this event is happening.

5. When the bell ran, we went to our bus. _____

Name: _____

Circle the words that name something (nouns)

1. letter   hurry   cupcake   pizza   wash

Correct these sentences.

2. dads knew car have a flate tire

_____

3. hims well hafta gets it fixed soone

_____

Real or make-believe?

4. Every time it snows, we don't go to school. _____

5. If there is an ice storm, roads are very slippery. _____

- -

Name: _____

Correct these sentences.

1. cats rabbits and hamsters has vary soft fur

_____

2. them can be meny differant colours two

_____

Write "g" or "j" to tell the sound of "g" in these words.

3. germ   _____

4. glow   _____

Circle the word that means more than one man.

5. mans   mens   men   means

SSR1145 ISBN: 9781771587310 © On The Mark Press

Name: _____

Write the correct word on each line name these groups.

school	flock	fleet	herd	team

1. a _____ of fish

2. a _____ of soccer players

3. a _____ of ships

4. a _____ of birds

5. a _____ of cows

Name: _____

Bonus Activity: Goodie Foodie

Unscramble the words to make the name of a Good Food snack. Write your answer under the picture.

selppa	sechee	leryec	rotracs	warsierebrst

MY CANADA

Why did the farmer call the vet for his cow? Because she was so mooo-dy.

Write the two words that make up each compound word.

1. outdoors _____

2. clubhouse _____

Circle the word that comes first alphabetically.

3. into   indeed   include   ink

Correct these sentences.

4. looks out for that there big puddle

_____

5. my pet kittan are black and whit

_____

Tell how many syllables are in this word.

1. wonderful _____

Write the pronoun for the underlined words.

2. Popcorn is my favourite treat. _____

3. My sister and I get it every time we go to a movie. _____

Correct these sentences.

4. i want to the park with janie sally and marie

_____

5. we played tage for too hours

_____

SSR1145   ISBN: 9781771587310 © On The Mark Press

Name: _____

Complete these analogies.

1. Fur is to cat as feathers are to _____

2. Pumpkin is to vine as apple is to _____

Circle the words that go together.

3. beaver   raccoon   eagle   chipmunk   duck

Correct these sentences.

4. we is geting ready for the terry fox run

_____

5. it are gonna bee on sunday september 17 2017

_____

- -

Name: _____

Tell what this person's job would be.

1. She cleans and fixes our teeth. _____

Correct these sentences.

2. gerry ask me too hims bertday party

_____

3. we is gonna go bowling and to sam's snacks for treets

_____

Explain the meaning of the underlined words.

4. You need to wash your hands. They are <u>filthy</u>._____

5. We <u>probably</u> will go to the movie tonight._____

Place the correct punctuation in these sentences. Use a period, question mark, exclamation mark or comma.

1. Patti Wendy and I are going to the beach

2. We are taking sandwiches drinks and cupcakes to eat

3. We need shovels pails and pretty stones to build a sand castle

4. We were proud of our castle It looked great

5. Do you like to build sand castles We do

Bonus Activity: Just Like the Animals

Write the correct animal name in the space. Then draw a picture of your answer.

mule   mouse   bear   fish

1. as quiet as a _____	2. swims like a _____
3. stubborn as a_____	4. hungry as a _____

MY CANADA

The world's largest beaver dam is in Northern Alberta.

SSR1145   ISBN: 9781771587310 © On The Mark Press

Name: _____

Correct these sentences.

1. i'm hungry i need a snack said lila

_____

2. why dont you has a apple i replied

_____

Explain the meaning of the underlined word.

3. This fairy tale tells about an <u>ogre</u>.

_____

Write the correct word on the line.

4. That is _____ hockey stick.   **Colins / Colin's / Colin**

5. _____ mom is a doctor.   **Fanny / Fannys / Fanny's**

- -

Name: _____

Correct these sentences.

1. did mr murrays dog have seven puppys

_____

2. whats he gonna do with so meny puppys

_____

Circle the words that are nouns.

3. We sat under the tree to eat our lunch.

4. My sister brought her doll to school.

Write the contraction made from these two words.

5. they are _____

Name: _____

Correct these sentences.

1. jackson are on the same teem as willy ted and seth

_____

2. them played a good game last saturday in danville park

_____

Circle the words that are opposites

3. harder   taller   softer   cleaner

Real or make-believe?

4. Fruits are good for us. _____

5. Bananas grow in Ontario. _____

- -

Name: _____

Circle the correct greeting.

1. Dear Aunt Susie   Dear, Aunt Susie   Dear Aunt Susie,

How do you spell the word meaning more than one?

2. baby   _____

3. fox   _____

Correct these sentences.

4. who winned the publick speaking contest

_____

5. me thinks it were that there knew girl lynne

_____

SSR1145   ISBN: 9781771587310 © On The Mark Press

Name: _____

A verb in the <u>present</u> is action <u>happening right now.</u>

A verb in the <u>past</u> is action that has <u>already finished.</u>

Write the correct verb on the line.

1. Last week, a police officer _____ our classroom.   **visited / visits**

2. I _____ it when a guest comes to our school.   **like / liked**

3. She _____ about how we can keep safe.   **talk / talked**

4. Ms Harris _____ the officer for coming.   **thanked / thank**

5. I _____ we have another visitor soon.   **hoped / hope**

Name: _____

Bonus Activity: Weather Words

Colour all the Weather Words light blue.

frost	rock	sleet	train	lightning
snow	tree	cloudy	sled	fog
rain	sunny	thunder	birds	flurries
storm	flower	blizzard	bees	drizzle
windy	car	hail	shark	mist

Who was Canada's first Prime Minister?   **MY CANADA**

Sir John A. Macdonald

Name: _____

Underline the words that tell why Joey began to cry.

1.   Joey began to cry when he broke his new toy truck.

Correct these sentences.

2.   did her give them cookys to her frend ruby

_____

3.   mrs adams rided the buss home frum work

_____

Complete the analogies.

4.   bear is to growl as dog is to _____

5.   blue is to sky as green is to _____

- -

Name: _____

Circle the word that means more than one.

1.   goose   gooses   geese

2.   mouses   mice   meese

Correct these sentences.

3.   dr barton live in a big house in the country

_____

4.   him is a vet who look after farm anamals

_____

Tell if this sentence is a *statement, question, exclamation* or *command*.

5.   Clean up that mess before you go outside. _____

        SSR1145   ISBN: 9781771587310 © On The Mark Press

Real or make-believe?

1. I saw an elf playing in the garden. _____

Correct these sentences.

2. does you likes ketchup and mutard on yur hot dogs

_____

3. me thinks karl breaked hims glasses

_____

Write the pronoun that would replace the underlined noun.

4. <u>My brother and I</u> are staying home tonight.   _____

5. <u>Mom and Dad are</u> going out for dinner.   _____

- -

Correct these sentences.

1. how did marc lost hims hat and mittens

_____

2. mike guy and larry feeded peenuts to them squirrels

_____

Write the correct abbreviation for each word.

3. street   _____

4. September   _____

Tell if the underlined word is a *noun* or *verb*

5. The <u>stars</u> are shining brightly tonight. _____

What Happens Next?

Circle what will happen next.

1. The telephone began to ring.
   (a) I will go to the door.   (b) I will answer it.

2. Jay dropped the glass and broke it.
   (a) He will tell his mom.   (b) He will run away.

3. Mother Hen sat on the eggs for days.
   (a) She threw away the shells.   (b) The chicks hatched.

4. After the rain, the sun was shining.
   (a) We saw a rainbow.   (b) Snow began to fall.

5. I got a great book at the library.
   (a) I will put it under my bed.   (b) I will start to read it.

Bonus Activity: Great Covers!

Read the titles of these books. Choose the sentence that tells what the book is about. Illustrate the covers.

Camping Adventures	Cooking for Kids	Canadian Trees
1. This book tells which animals live in the woods.	1. This book has ideas for foods kids can cook.	1. This book tells facts about Canada's trees.
2. This book tells how to have fun camping.	2. This book tells you where to shop.	2. This book tells us about good fishing spots.

Where do Snow People keep their money? In a Snow Bank!

MY CANADA

SSR1145   ISBN: 9781771587310 © On The Mark Press

Name: _____

Correct these sentences.

1. me and addie cant go to the halloween party

_____

2. i doesnt like turnip beets or carots

_____

Circle the adjectives in each sentence.

3. That small brown button fell off his coat.

4. We rolled big snowballs to make that giant snowfort.

Write the correct word on the line.

5. What are _____ going to do on Saturday?

them / there / they

- -

Name: _____

Correct these sentences.

1. she has went shoppin with hers aunt libby

_____

2. i thinks they has gone to the yorkdale mall

_____

Is this sentence a *statement, question, command* or *exclamation*?

3. Hurray Our team won _____

How many syllables in each word?

4. New Brunswick _____

5. Saskatchewan _____

WEEK
25

ACTIVITY
3

TOTAL
/5

Common or proper noun?

1.   CN Tower   _____

2.   railroad   _____

Correct these sentences.

3.   edna finded for easter eggs under hers bed

_____

4.   how did bernie gets all them right answers

_____

Number these words in alphabetical order.

5.   ___ eagle   ___ egg   ___ eel   ___ empty   ___ elk

- -

WEEK
25

ACTIVITY
4

TOTAL
/5

Correct these sentences.

1.   gimme a cooky and a glas of milke

_____

2.   we beginned to washe the dishs after dinner

_____

Circle the words that mean the same as "big".

3.   huge   tiny   large   empty

Sentence or not a sentence?

4.   The best sport   _____

5.   I love poutine!   _____

   SSR1145   ISBN: 9781771587310 © On The Mark Press

Dear grandpa

can i come to your house this weekend Maybe we cood go fishin i wood love fish for supper

love brad

_____

_____

_____

_____

_____

_____

Bonus Activity: Homophones

Homophones are words that sound alike but have different *meanings* and *spellings*.

Circle the correct word that matches the picture. In the last box, pick one homophone and draw its picture in the box.

hair hare	bawl ball	son sun	whale wail	pair pear

*The **toque** was invented in Canada over 400 years ago.*

MY CANADA

SSR1145   ISBN: 9781771587310 © On The Mark Press

Name: _____

Write present or past to tell when these things happened.

1. I had fun playing at Jake's house last Saturday. _____

2. Let's set the table for dinner. _____

Correct these sentences.

3. them boys was runnin and jumpin and laughin

_____

4. hank digged a whol to plant hims littel tree

_____

Complete the following analogy.

5. 7 is to number as M is to _____

- -

Name: _____

Same or opposite?

1. start, begin _____

2. prince, princess _____

How many syllables?

3. mountain goat _____

Correct these sentences.

4. mrs carter told us a funy story about a baby bare

_____

5. this here bare liked to pick berrys to eats

_____

    SSR1145   ISBN: 9781771587310 © On The Mark Press

Name: _____

Write the pronoun that would replace the underlined words.

1. Jack and Jill went up the hill. _____

2. The pail of water tumbled down the hill. _____

Correct these sentences.

3. our class are gonna go up in the cn tower

_____

4. well youse be afraide to go to the top

_____

Where does this happen?

5. The player hit a home run. _____

Name: _____

Correct these sentences.

1. wen can him and me play that there game

_____

2. do a spider has ate legs

_____

Write the correct word on the line.

3. John is _____ to the dentist tomorrow.
   go / gone / going

4. She will _____ at the concert on Sunday.
   sang / sing / sung

Circle the words that name insects.

5. bee   toad   wasp   ant   fish

Name: _____

Combining Sentences

Write one good sentence using these short sentences.

1. Grandma baked cookies. Grandma baked muffins.

_____

2. My aunt loves books. My aunt loves movies.

_____

3. The dog barked. The dog wagged its tail.

_____

4. Dad started the lawnmower. Dad cut the grass.

_____

5. Donnie told a funny joke. We laughed at his joke.

_____

- -

Name: _____

Bonus Activity: Sh! Silent Letters

These words have silent consonants. Complete the puzzle by matching the words to its clue.

	knot	gnaw	knight	comb	knife	knock
Clue						
1. A dog does this to a bone.						
2. We use this for our hair.						
3. You can tie this in a rope.						
4. We use this to cut things.						
5.We do this on a door.						
6. I can fight battles and dragons.						

Who has won hockey gold more than any other country? Canada, of course!

MY CANADA

SSR1145   ISBN: 9781771587310 © On The Mark Press

Name: _____

Correct these sentences.

1. has you ever red <u>the night before christmas</u>

_____

2. he dont have no money left in hims piggy bank

_____

Write the two words that make up each contractions.

3. she'll _____

4. that's _____

Circle two words that have the same meaning.

5. joyful   sad   angry   happy

- -

Name: _____

Circle the plural form of each noun.

1. foot :   foots   feet   footes

2. child :   child   childrens   children

What caused Jules to break the glass? Underline your answer.

3. Jules dropped the glass and broke it.

Correct these sentences.

4. paige want to play withe bella and josie

_____

5. they is making up a play abut a magical hoarse

_____

Explain the meaning of the underlined words.

1. It is safe to swim in the <u>shallow</u> end of the pool. _____

2. Mosquitoes were a <u>nuisance</u> to us on our hike. _____

Correct these sentences.

3. does you wants to go to summer camp

_____

4. i goes to camp wellwood evry summer in july

_____

Circle the word that is an adjective.

5. nurse   hurry   clean   time

Write three words that rhyme with "glow"

1. glow: _____

Correct these sentences.

2. a mouse runned fast acrost our flore

_____

3. then it runned under my bed and hided

_____

Circle the nouns in each sentence.

4. The world's largest bird is an ostrich.

5. Gina can play the piano and the harp.

SSR1145   ISBN: 9781771587310 © On The Mark Press

Name: _____

Write the correct word on each line.

1. Jacko is the _____ parrot in the pet shop.

   smart / smarter / smartest

2. Bill is tall but his brother is _____

   tall / taller / tallest

3. Maggy loves chocolate ice cream the _____

   good / better / best

4. David runs _____ than I run.

   quick / quicker / quickest

5. The Smith children live _____ the school.

   near / nearer / nearest

Name: _____

Bonus Activity: Growing in Canada, You will Find ....

Find and circle the following words in the puzzle.

ash	apple	birch	cedar	elm	maple	oak	pine	spruce	willow
w	c	e	m	a	p	l	e	s	h
c	i	b	e	d	f	l	g	p	i
a	d	l	y	w	p	s	k	r	o
e	m	z	l	p	x	i	l	u	j
b	a	k	a	o	f	u	n	c	n
k	i	h	g	a	w	v	m	e	p
m	h	j	n	s	o	t	s	q	r
b	i	r	c	h	r	a	d	e	c

Which Great Lake might be home to a ghost? Lake Erie! **MY CANADA**

Name: _____

Put the apostrophe (') in the correct place

1. Davids football

2. the girls bicycles

Correct these sentences.

3. is you gonna come shoppin with use

_____

4. we is gonna go erly on saturday morning

_____

Did this happen in the present or in the past?

5. Timmy went camping last weekend at Sand Lake. _____

- -

Name: _____

Where would the following probably take place?

1. Get your ticket and line up for the ride. _____

Correct these sentences.

2. aunt kamis presant arrived on may 21 2012

_____

3. how meny childrens was at yore party

_____

Real or make-believe?

4. Robins make their nests in trees. _____

5. Cats that are pets will not chase birds. _____

SSR1145   ISBN: 9781771587310 © On The Mark Press

Name: _____

Statement or question?

1.   Did dinosaurs ever live in Alberta   _____

2.   Scientists have found many bones there   _____

Circle the words that have the sound of "g" in "get"

3.   gum   giant   going   gem   gate

Correct the following sentences.

4.   why wasnt you eating them cookys

_____

5.   my frends les and luke is twins

_____

- -

Name: _____

Complete the analogy.

1.   cow is to moo as cat is to _____

Correct these sentences.

2.   him and me went bikeing to that there park

_____

3.   whats the bestest game to play indoors

_____

Circle the adverbs (describes action) in these sentences.

4.   She screamed loudly when she saw the bug.

_____

5.   The fish flopped wildly on the hook.

_____

Name: _____

Read each sentence. Put in the end punctuation. Then tell the kind of sentence.

ACTIVITY 5

Write S for Statement; Q for Question; C for Command; and E for Exclamation.

TOTAL /5

1. I have a secret to tell you _____

2. Do you promise not to tell anyone _____

3. Tomorrow is my birthday _____

4. Hooray, it's finally here _____

5. Come to my house on Saturday to my party _____

Name: _____

Bonus Activity: Snow Day!

BONUS! ACTIVITY

Bad weather often means a Snow Day for Canadian children. Number these sentences in the order that they happened.

_____ They made a big snowman in their backyard.

_____ In the morning, Max looked out the window.

_____ Max and his sister went outside to play.

_____ It snowed and snowed all night.

_____ "School buses are cancelled today," said Mom.

A Canadian invented the 3D jigsaw puzzle.

MY CANADA

  SSR1145   ISBN: 9781771587310 © On The Mark Press

Name: _____

Correct these sentences.

1. can you till ant beth i well visit on sunday

_____

2. if you clime that tree, dont fell

_____

Tell if the word means one or more than one.

3. teeth _____

4. helmet _____

Command, exclamation, question, or statement?

5. Study your words for your spelling test. _____

- -

Name: _____

Correct these sentences.

1. did her remember too take her too books to school

_____

2. i wants too read the poem <u>alligator pie</u>

_____

Write the correct verb on the line.

3. We all _____ for the singer.

   clap / clapping / clapped

4. Dad is _____ in the big race.

   run/ running / ran

Circle the word that needs an apostrophe.

5. Marys   kiss   reads   washes

Correct these sentences.

1. who is gonna be yur knew techer

   _____

2. me thinks it well bee mr gordon

   _____

Common **or** *proper noun*?

3. Nova Scotia   _____

4. tides   _____

Circle the adjectives in this sentence.

5. Spud is a brown and white bulldog. _____

Write the root or base word for these words.

1. closest   _____

2. skipping   _____

Correct these sentences.

3. gimme a glass of colde water, plese

   _____

4. them cats is goode at catching mouses

   _____

How many syllables?

5. Vancouver Island   _____

SSR1145   ISBN: 9781771587310 © On The Mark Press

Name: _____

Homophones

Write the correct homophone on the line.

1. I _____ out invitations to my birthday party.

    scent / sent

2. I was allowed to invite _____ friends.

    four / for

3. If it doesn't _____ we are going on a hike.

    rain / rein

4. We will go by an old cabin made of _____

    would / wood

5. Last week, dad and I saw two _____ near the cabin.

    dear / deer

Name: _____

Bonus Activity: I Love the Beach!

Read these words that tell about <u>things to take</u> or <u>things to do</u> at the beach.

If the word is a <u>noun</u> (names something), colour the box <u>yellow.</u> If the word is a <u>verb</u> (action), colour the box <u>blue</u>.

swimsuit	dig	play	swim
hat	beach towel	shovel	run
sandwiches	build	snacks	sunglasses

Five-pin bowling was invented in Canada in 1908.

MY CANADA

Real or make-believe?

1. A beaver's home is called a lodge. _____

Correct these sentences.

2. whin is you koming to sea me

_____

3. wee can has a sleep over in my tent

_____

Circle the word that does not belong in the group.

4. bears   elephants   apples   monkeys   lions

5. yellow   red   orange   circle   green

Same or opposite?

1. cry, laugh _____

Correct these sentences.

2. was there aunts on the picnic table asked cam

_____

3. no, i skared thems all away, said maggy

_____

Write the number of syllables in each word.

4. colourful _____

5. Summerside _____

SSR1145   ISBN: 9781771587310 © On The Mark Press

Correct these sentences.

1. him just lerned to rid hims knew bike

_____

2. who is gonna help my make me bed

_____

Circle the word that comes first in alphabetical order.

3. x-ray   queen   very   zebra   window

Circle the words that are spelled correctly.

4. ar   oure   our   owr   ower

5. whut   wat   waht   what   wath

- -

Correct these sentences.

1. wee liked the story <u>the littlest dragon</u>

_____

2. ms dawson readed it to us last weak

_____

Circle the words that mean the same thing.

3. sad   happy   merry   sick   glad

Write the contraction made from these words.

4. will not _____

5. is not _____

Name: _____

Object pronouns take the place of the object in a sentence.

Object pronouns are: *me, you, her, him, them, us, it.*

Write the object pronoun that could replace the underlined word.

1. Kelly gave <u>Kim</u> some of her popcorn. _____

2. I ride on <u>a bus</u> to school. _____

3. We cheered for <u>Ronnie and David</u> to win the race. _____

4. Mrs. Hartley gave <u>my class</u> a treat. _____

5. Did you see <u>the rainbow</u> yesterday? _____

- -

Name: _____

Bonus Activity: Make New Words

Change around the letters in each word to match the clue.

1. Change <u>notes</u> into a small rock. _____

2. Change <u>lump</u> into a sweet, purple fruit. _____

3. Change <u>shore</u> into an animal a cowboy rides. _____

4. Change <u>swap</u> into an insect that will sting you. _____

5. Change <u>stool</u> into things we use for work. _____

What is often plowed but never planted? Snow!

MY CANADA

 SSR1145   ISBN: 9781771587310 © On The Mark Press

Name: _____

Circle the adjectives in each sentence.

1. That red van belongs to our new neighbour.

2. I love chocolate cake with white icing!

Correct these sentences.

3. bares eats lottsa food in the spring and simmer

_____

4. then them gose to sleep for the hole winter

_____

Write the correct word on the line.

5. Betty _____ when a mouse ran across the floor.

    scream / screaming / screamed

Name: _____

Write the two words that make up each compound word.

1. buttercup   _____

2. basketball   _____

Correct these sentences.

3. my frend, bruce, and me likes to doe the same things

_____

4. sometimes us play basball feetball or golfe

_____

Underline the part that tells what happened when it started to rain.

5. We ran inside when it started to rain.

Name: _____

Circle the word that does not belong in each group.

1. apples   oranges   lemons   cars   plums

2. candles   cake   squirrels   presents   friends

How many syllables?

3. grandfather _____

Correct these sentences.

4. little miss muffet sat on her tuffet to ate

_____

5. a big black hairy spider skared she away

_____

Name: _____

Circle the adverbs in this sentence.

1. Yesterday I ran home quickly.

Correct these sentences.

2. hims pet rabbit are named boomer

_____

3. aint that a funy name fer a pet rabbit

_____

Sentence or not a sentence?

4. Stand right here _____

5. All alone _____

 SSR1145   ISBN: 9781771587310 © On The Mark Press

Name: _____

We use commas between things in a list. Put the commas where they belong in each sentence.

1. Dale Matt Hal and Nate are playing a game.

2. It snowed on Saturday Sunday Monday and Tuesday.

3. My family likes to skate toboggan ski and sled.

4. Her favourite snacks are cookies apples carrots and chips.

5. In school, we study math science reading and music.

Name: _____

Bonus Activity:

Read the sentences that make up this story.

Illustrate each sentence in the box.

Write a good title for this story.

My title is _____

I have a pet hamster named Patches.	He likes to hide in the wood shavings.	He likes to stuff his cheeks with food.	At night, he runs and runs on his wheel.

MY CANADA

*The longest **skating rink** in the world is in Ottawa, Ontario.*

Correct these sentences.

1. what did that there man asks you

   _____

2. did them gerls go swimmin in the lake

   _____

Circle the words that rhyme with "good"

3. stood   flood   hood   mood

Same or opposite?

4. start   begin   _____

5. quick   slow   _____

WEEK
32

ACTIVITY
1

TOTAL
/5

What time of year might this take place?

1. The tulips started to bloom. _____

Correct these sentences.

2. wen i grow up, im gonna bee a doctor

   _____

3. the carpenter builded a fence outta bords

   _____

Underline the subject in each sentence.

4. All cats have whiskers.

5. Jessie hates dill pickles.

WEEK
32

ACTIVITY
2

TOTAL
/5

SSR1145   ISBN: 9781771587310 © On The Mark Press

Name: _____

Sentence or not a sentence?

1. The oldest boy. _____

2. My mother called me. _____

Correct these sentences.

3. grandpa eat eggs bakon and taost for brekfast

_____

4. clen up that there mess rite now

_____

Complete this analogy.

5. duck is to duckling as hen is to _____

- -

Name: _____

Write the word that means more than one "peach".

1. _____

Correct these sentences.

2. lets plante beens carrots and corn in our gardin

_____

3. alec and john is twins who lives next dore

_____

Write two words that rhyme with each word.

4. sheep _____

5. goat _____

Write the letter correctly on the lines below.

october 1 2017

dear joan

    wood you likes to come to my house for thanksgivin dinner my mom are cookin a big turkay she also will cook potaoes gravy carrots and corn we has punkin pie for dessert

your frend

patti

_____

_____

_____

Name: _____

Bonus Activity: A Not – So – Secret Message!

Discover the message by writing the letters in the boxes.

Write the letter that comes <u>before</u> each one you see.

The first one has been done to help you.

C														!
d	b	o	b	e	b	j	t	n	z	i	p	n	f	!

If you have a purple bill and a blue bill, how much money do you have? $15

MY CANADA

ANSWER KEY

WEEK 1: ACTIVITY 1

1. Dan and David are cousins.
2. Can you help me fix this?
3. (run)   down   (look)   tree
4. sad   baseball   (jog)   (cry)
5. Where is the soccer ball Question

WEEK 1: ACTIVITY 2

1. Each morning at breakfast Not a sentence
2. Look at the Canada goose Sentence
3. My library book is at school.
4. Did you see the rainbow in the sky?
5. leef   leafe   lefe   (leaf)

WEEK 1: ACTIVITY 3

1. (ontario)   forest   bear   (manitoba)
2. Wow, I won first prize!
3. Where are we going for lunch?
4. - ack family : back, hack, lack, Mack, pack, quack ...
5. - ight family : fight, light, might, night

WEEK 1: ACTIVITY 4

1. (book)   bark   (cook)   (shook)   lot
2. (wet)   (jet)   got   (pet)   cat.
3. Where are your new shoes?
4. We saw a chipmunk in the yard.
5. (city)   candy   (circle)   cake   (centre)

WEEK 1: ACTIVITY 5

*1. Do you have a pet ?
 2. I have a cat named Duffy .
 3. What a great idea !
*4. Do you want to play baseball with us ?
 5. I love to play Lego with my friends .

BONUS ACTIVITY: SOMETHING FISHY!

				t	p		s
c			u		e		m
	o	n			r		e
h	a	d	d	o	c	k	l
	s				h		t
		o					
	s	a	l	m	o	n	
g	n	i	r	r	e	h	

WEEK 2: ACTIVITY 1

1. Are they going to move away?
2. Mom and I are going shopping on Saturday.
3. canoe 2
4. summertime 3
5. I am   I'm

Week 2: Activity 2

1. Back on the shelf.   Sentence   (Not a sentence)
2. Take the dog for a walk.   (Sentence)   Not a sentence
3. Canada has four seasons   Real
4. The fox lives in a den in the field.
5. How many fox pups live with the mother?

Week 2: Activity 3

1. ice cream cone   Popsicle   ice cream sandwich
   Hot weather treats
2. Let's go catch some fish for dinner.
3. We can cook them in the frying pan.
4. Hen is to egg as cow is to : milk
5. Girl is to woman as boy is to : man

Week 2: Activity 4

1. When is Harry getting his new puppy?
2. Sally and I like to skip.
3. -ill : bill, dill, fill, gill, hill, Jill, kill ...
4. lunch   (b) a meal eaten at noon
5. dance   (c) to move in time to music

Week 2: Activity 5   Nouns Name Things

book	boy	beach	baby	bat

What is true about each word?   Each word begins with "b"

Bonus Activity: Rhyming Riddles

Rhyming Clue	Meaning	New Word	My Picture
Rhymes with "dug"	An insect	bug	
Rhymes with "bake"	Something good to eat	cake	
Rhymes with "wish"	It swims in a lake	fish	
Rhymes with "boy"	Something to play with	toy	

Week 3: Activity 1

1. Those clowns did funny tricks at the circus.
2. Jenny ran fast to win the race.
3. sunshine : sun + shine
4. outside : out + side
5. ghost   bank   candy   (apple)   home

Week 3: Activity 2

1. A picnic on Sunday.   Not a sentence
2. We are going to see Grandma.   Sentence
3. My friend, Damon, wasn't at school today.
4. I helped Uncle Jack milk the cows.
5. Fry.   Frid.   (Fri.)   Fr.

Week 3: Activity 3

1. four   (hockey)   eight   three
2. hamster   puppy   (cookie)   pony
3. Tom gave Charlie his best ball glove.
4. When is our class trip to Montreal?
5. There is a pot of gold at the end of a
   rainbow.   Make-believe

Week 3: Activity 4

1. I love chocolate ice cream!   Verb
2. The mother lion looks after her cubs.   Noun
3. We are going sailing on the St. Lawrence River.
4. Has the Brown family moved away yet?
5. (sale)   saile   salle   sile

Week 3: Activity 5

1. pencil : pencils
2. dish : dishes
3. chair : chairs
4. fox : foxes
5. patch : patches

 SSR1145   ISBN: 9781771587310 © On The Mark Press

Bonus Activity: Giving Thanks

1. F   Thanksgiving is celebrated in November.
2. T   Pioneer families started the first Thanksgiving.
3. T   Today we have a big dinner with our family and friends.

Week 4: Activity 1

1. Did she break that glass dish?
2. Dad and I went fishing for perch.
3. 2 jam   3 rattle   1 happy   4 summer
4. raccoon : 2
5. Vancouver : 3

Week 4: Activity 2

1. huge   glad   (tiny)   slow
2. baseball : base + ball
3. snowshoe : snow + shoe
4. Mother cat hid her kittens in the barn.
5. Did your mom make those cookies?

Week 4: Activity 3

1. Thanksgiving   Christmas   (Toronto)   Easter
2. blue   purple   (sunny)   green
3. Did you learn how to skate last year?
4. I'll ask my dad if i can go with you.
5. - ing : bring, ding, ring, sing, fling...

Week 4: Activity 4

1. wiht   wif   (with)   withe
2. bute   (but)   bote   botte
3. We saw a lot of mice in the old shed.
4. Do you think our cat, Sally, can catch them?
5. Novem.   Novemb.   Novmbr.   (Nov.)

Week 4: Activity 5

1. Do you have a new kitten?   Question
2. I saw a gorilla at the zoo.   Statement]
3. I like the movie called Zootopia .   Statement
4. Have you seen it yet ?   Question
5. Next week I am going to Winnipeg .   Statement

Bonus Activity: Weather Nouns

	Clue					
1	You can make a snow-fort with me.	s	n	o	w	*	*
2	You will get wet when I fall on you.	r	a	i	n	*	*
3	I am a balls of ice that fall to earth,	h	a	i	l	*	*
4	I can be strong or gentle when I blow.	w	i	n	d	*	*
5	I can be white and fluffy or very dark.	c	l	o	u	d	*

Week 5: Activity 1

1. children More than one
2. Did your baby brother take your cookie?
3. I saw a rainbow in the sky today.
4. Are you a good soccer player Question
5. Hurrah, I won Exclamation

Week 5: Activity 2

1. You can spin straw into gold.   Make-believe
2. Fishermen catch lobsters in traps.   Real
3. Marty lives in Langley, British Columbia.
4. Are you going in the Terry Fox Run?
5. camper : campers

WEEK 5: ACTIVITY 3

1. Theo is the <u>fastest</u> runner in our class.
2. Today is <u>sunnier</u> than yesterday.
3. 2   bet   1   bat   4   but   3   bit
4. Please be on time for our game on Saturday.
5. Bring your lunch, a water bottle, and sunscreen.

WEEK 5: ACTIVITY 4

1. Ontario : 4
2. We're going to Nova Scotia in August.
3. Are you going to visit your Aunt Betty?
4. bee is to hive as bird is to : nest
5. duck is to duckling as hen is to : chick

WEEK 5: ACTIVITY 5 TRICKY NOUNS

1. baby : babies
2. story : stories
3. foot : feet
4. child : children
5. man : men

BONUS ACTIVITY: HOMOPHONES

*deer	*pear	*8	*pail	*toe	*1
deer	pear	eight	pail	toe	one

WEEK 6: ACTIVITY 1

1. Terry went fishing in the pond.
2. Did he catch any fish to eat?
3. I (am) going to the Calgary Stampede.
4. We (are) going this summer.
5. don't : do not   that's : that is

WEEK 6: ACTIVITY 2

1. new, pew, stew, glue, blue ....
2. Jackie swung the bat as hard as he could.   Playing baseball
3. Wes climbed to the top, sat down, and slid to the ground.   Going down a slide
4. Our cat ran after the mice.
5. She likes to show me when she catches one.

WEEK 6: ACTIVITY 3

1. - oi : boil, coil, foil, oil, toil
2. The children (splashed) around in the pool..
3. Sammy (named) his duck Little Peep.
4. Have you ever read the book <u>Flat Stanley</u> ?
5. How many sheep are in the pen?

WEEK 6: ACTIVITY 4

1. Don't you have any cookies to share?
2. This game is fun to play.
3. Made a birthday cake.   Not a sentence
4. My sister's birthday is on Sunday.   sentence
5. (david) is playing soccer for the (rosetown) (runners).

WEEK 6: ACTIVITY 5

1. Can you hear the wolves <u>howl</u> at night?
2. I will <u>help</u> Mom do the dishes.
3. Lions <u>roar</u> to scare their enemies.
4. Here <u>comes</u> the Canada Day parade!
5. Grant <u>scores</u> the most goals in hockey.

BONUS ACTIVITY: ANIMAL CATEGORIES

Birds	Fish	Mammals	Reptiles
loon	tuna	bear	snake
blue jay	cod	raccoon	salamander
goose	haddock	beaver	lizard

WEEK 7: ACTIVITY 1

1. Our dog, Jake, needed a bath last night.
2. He was running through mud puddles.
3. That was a (funney) story we read.
4. May I play (wiht) you and your team?
5. Only boys play hockey.   Make-believe

WEEK 7: ACTIVITY 2

1. box : boxes
2. lady : ladies
3. dull : sharp, shiny
4. My little sister is two years old in April.
5. Ms Hunt read <u>Anne of Green Gables</u> to our class.

SSR1145   ISBN: 9781771587310 © On The Mark Press

Week 7: Activity 3

1. lake   pond   mountain   river
2. Why are we staying home this weekend?
3. You need to clean your room.
4. Toronto : 3
5. Rocky Mountains : 4

Week 7: Activity 4

1. Andy and Luke weren't at school today.
2. Molly was surprised when she got a new puppy.
3. babies   leaves   feet
4. the hat of my Grandpa : my Grandpa's hat
5. the friend of Kenny : Kenny's friend

Week 7: Activity 5   Contractions in Sentences

1. They've been playing baseball all day.
2. Who 's going to be on our team?
3. Aren't you coming with us to the beach?
4. We're going to swim and have a picnic.
5. Let's invite Roger and Abi to come with us.

Bonus Activity: Crack the Code

23	8	1	20		3	15	12	15	21	18		9	19		15	21	18		6	12	1	7	
w	h	a	t		c	o	l	o	u	r		i	s		o	u	r		f	l	a	g	?

My answer is : red and white

Week 8: Activity 1

1. That's the smallest kitten I have ever seen.
2. Allan went to see Dr. Hardy.
3. fireplace : fire + place
4. sailboat : sail + boat
5. Hamilton, Ontario

Week 8: Activity 2

1. Bobby (ran) down the lane and (jumped) over the fence.
2. Callie (cried) when she (lost) her jacket.
3. white
4. I'll help you clean your room today.
5. What's your favourite snack for school?

Week 8: Activity 3

1. Montreal : city
2. Toronto Blue Jays : baseball team.
3. Can you sing the song "Rain, Rain, Go Away"?
4. My favourite foods are pizza, milk, and ice cream.
5. Close the gate and lock it.   command

Week 8: Activity 4

1. Jeff's dad took the car to wash it.
2. We need to hurry or we'll miss the bus.
3. That's the best chocolate cake in the world!
4. tooth + brush = toothbrush
5. rain + coat = raincoat

Week 8: Activity 5

1. My favourite ice cream is chocolate.
2. Those black lab puppies are cute.
3. I am having a birthday party on Saturday.
4. We played a game of ball in the backyard.
5. Aunt Jane is coming tomorrow from Moncton.

Bonus Activity: Colour Unscramble

*yellow	*green	*purple	*blue	*orange	*brown

Week 9: Activity 1

1. sunny : cloudy
2. strong : weak, feeble
3. Were you following that path through the woods?
4. There weren't any cookies in the jar.
5. city   cereal   circle

Week 9: Activity 2

1. cherries
2. men
3. Penguins live in Canada's Arctic.   Make-believe
4. There are four blue eggs in that nest.
5. When will those eggs hatch?

SSR1145   ISBN: 9781771587310 © On The Mark Press

WEEK 9: ACTIVITY 3

1. (Harriet and her sister) want a goldfish for a pet.
2. Did all those apples fall from that tree?
3. Dad took us to Niagara Falls.
4. Wonderland : 3
5. ferris wheel : 3

WEEK 9: ACTIVITY 4

1. Josh lost two teeth this week.
2. Do you live in Alberta, Ontario, or Quebec?
3. We found an old trunk in the attic. A large box used for storing things
4. We played games and had cake and ice cream. At a (birthday) party
5. Kelly built a big sand castle. At the beach; in a sandbox

WEEK 9: ACTIVITY 5

Dear Logan,
　　Can you come to my house on Friday night? You and I will have fun playing Lego.

Bye for now
Reese

BONUS ACTIVITY: DOUBLE, DOUBLE

1. I love to chew bubble gum!
2. Those clouds are white and fluffy.
3. My favourite season is summer.
4. Dad lets me paddle our canoe.
5. I like people with good manners.

WEEK 10: ACTIVITY 1

1. - ate : date, fate, gate, hate, late, mate ...
2. - ue : blue, due, hue, clue, glue ...
3. Why were the boys running away from you?
4. Toby sang a song all by himself.
5. King is to prince as queen is to : princess

WEEK 10: ACTIVITY 2

1. Gary (laughed) at the funny clown.
2. The wind (blew) hard all night long.
3. boys
4. Have you read the story Goodnight, Mr. Moon?
5. We don't go to school in July or August.

WEEK 10: ACTIVITY 3

1. 2 bear　　3 bite　　1 bake　　4 bottle
2. How big are Wally's new soccer shoes?
3. It might rain so take your umbrella.
4. The (clown) had a big red (nose).
5. Are the (boys) running in this (race)?

WEEK 10 :ACTIVITY 4

1. Wasn't that the funniest story you (have) ever heard?
2. Didn't you bring those treats for us?
3. shakes : bakes, cakes, makes, flakes, quakes ...
4. Mary rode her bike home.　　She
5. We laughed at the joke.　　it

WEEK 10: ACTIVITY 5

1. A big plane flew over my house.
2. We are having hot dogs and hamburgers tonight.
3. Did Harry go swimming in the lake?
4. I have math homework to do.
5. A robin is in the birdbath.

BONUS ACTIVITY

h	g	i	h				
s	i	g	h				t
t	h	g	i	f			h
	n	t	h	g	i	r	g
		i		w			i
			g		a		s
	m	i	g	h	t	y	
				t			

SSR1145　ISBN: 9781771587310 © On The Mark Press

WEEK 11: ACTIVITY 1

1. I have a sandwich and two cookies in my lunch.
2. Do you like chocolate milk or white milk?
3. cry: dry, fry, try, my, why ...
4. flew: blew, brew, knew, grew, screw...
5. We are going to the beach.

WEEK 11: ACTIVITY 2

1. Snowed all day   Not a sentence
2. We built a snowfort in the yard.   Sentence
3. Aunt Darlene cooked a turkey for Sunday dinner.
4. Mark and I ate a big drumstick all by ourselves.
5. bicycle 3

WEEK 11: ACTIVITY 3

1 Sonya and I were laughing at the funny show.
2. It was about a talking cow named Daisy.
3. (Amy) loves to draw and colour.
4. (Cheese) is a healthy snack.
5. George is the tallest boy in my class.

WEEK 11: ACTIVITY 4

1. The sky can look red in a sunset.   Real
2. Some beans can grow a giant beanstalk.   Make-believe
3. Don't put those dirty shoes on the clean floor.
4. Why don't you wipe them off outside?
5. We (shouted) and (cheered) for the home team.

WEEK 11: ACTIVITY 5

1. I am going to build a farm with my Lego.
2. Of all my toys, I like Lego the best.
3. Sometimes I sit and play with it for hours.
4. I heard there is a new set with animals.
5. I am going to ask my mom to buy that set for my birthday.

BONUS ACTIVITY: ACTION WORD PUZZLE

Word Clues: You do this ---					
1. if you are in a race.	r	u	n	*	*
2. with a song.	s	i	n	g	*
3. with a book.	r	e	a	d	*
4. to make a picture.	d	r	a	w	*
5. to get to the top of a hill.	c	l	i	m	b
6. when something is funny.	l	a	u	g	h

WEEK 12: ACTIVITY 1

1. Jack was as hungry as a bear.   Jack was very hungry.
2. Annie's birthday is on Monday, August 21.
3. Are you going to go to her birthday party?
4. Sammy and Sue have a new pug puppy.   They
5. Their puppy follows them everywhere.   It

WEEK 12: ACTIVITY 2

1. Those socks are too small for my feet.
2. Do you have a pair I could borrow?
3. laughing
4. drink
5. coat, goat. float, moat

WEEK 12: ACTIVITY 3

1. My sister and I like to play in the sand.
2. We built a huge sand castle with two towers.
3. We (skated for three hours on the pond.)
4. We (drank hot chocolate to warm up.)
5. Toronto Raptors   Proper noun

WEEK 12: ACTIVITY 4

1. Don't step in that puddle.
2. Aren't you wearing your new shoes?
3. don't : do not
4. I'm : I am
5. ...2.. belt   ..3... bolt   ...1.. baby   ...4. burn

WEEK 12: ACTIVITY 5

1. They <u>are</u> going to the circus on Saturday.
2. Logan <u>doesn't</u> know the answer to that question.
3. Mom <u>made</u> spaghetti for supper last night.
4. Our class <u>is</u> singing a song at the concert.
5. We <u>don't</u> want to stay home from the movie.

BONUS ACTIVITY: THE LONG AND SHORT OF IT

pen (Y)	mice (G)	tub (Y)	cane (G)
came (G)	rat (Y)	jet (Y)	rule (G)
mule (G)	nine (G)	cake (G)	top (Y)

WEEK 13: ACTIVITY 1

1. sleep   talk   work   (walk)   sing
2. Do you like apples, oranges, and grapes?
3. Those boys didn't do anything bad.
4. somewhere
5. snowman

WEEK 13: ACTIVITY 2

1. sick : well, healthy
2. near : far, distant
3. Does Jenny live on Main Street?
4. Yes, she lives at 205 Main Street.
5. A flock of Canada <u>geese</u> flew high in the sky.

WEEK 13: ACTIVITY 3

1. Molly has a new <u>pair</u> of shoes.   (b) two of something
2. Have you heard the song called <u>Twinkle, Twinkle, Little Star</u> ?
3. Many children know that song.
4. down
5. town

WEEK 13: ACTIVITY 4

1. "What would you like for lunch?" asked Tom.
2. Willy is taking his dog, Barney, for a walk.
3. Barney likes to roll in the grass and the mud.
4. bringing : bring
5. getting : get

WEEK 13: ACTIVITY 5

...4... We are all packed for the trip.
...2... Mom and Dad said I could ask a friend to go.
...1... We are going on a short vacation.
...3... I am taking my pal, Shelby.
...5.. I am really excited to be going.

BONUS ACTIVITY: ODD WORD OUT

bacon	eggs	toast	(pencil)	milk
soccer	basketball	baseball	swimming	(sweater)
pencil	eraser	ruler	(hammer)	paper
shoes	coat	(truck)	mittens	hat
cows	(books)	chickens	horses	pigs

WEEK 14: ACTIVITY 1

1. Ben didn't know the way to Kelly's house.
2. The hens on Grandpa's farm lay lots of eggs.
3. Edmonton 3
4. Vancouver Canucks hockey team
5. St. Lawrence river

WEEK 14: ACTIVITY 2

1. The best day of the year is July 1, 2017.
2. That's the day Canada will be 150 years old.
3. grow : blow, flow, glow, sow, mow ....
4. bright : light, fight, fright, might, night ....
5. skis   snowshoes   snowboard   sled   They are ways to travel on snow.

WEEK 14: ACTIVITY 3

1. should've : should have
2. I'll : I will / shall
3. Those bees were buzzing around the flowers in his garden.
4. He grows vegetables like carrots, beans, and corn.
5. dry   damp   Antonyms

WEEK 14: ACTIVITY 4

1. Will you help me build a snowfort in my yard?
2. It will make a good clubhouse for our friends.
3. <u>Dad</u> is making me a car for the soapbox derby.   He
4. <u>My car</u> will be red with orange and yellow flames.   It
5. The dog guards the <u>flock</u> of sheep to keep them safe.   A group or herd.

SSR1145   ISBN: 9781771587310 © On The Mark Press

Week 14: Activity 5

February 10, 2017.

Dear Ella

Family Day is coming soon. My mom says I can invite you over to our house. She will take us to Pizza Hut. Let me know if you can come.

Your friend,

Chloe

Bonus Activity: We Get Around

Land	Air	Water
car	jet	kayak
van	hot air balloon	jet ski
train	helicopter	canoe
bicycle	drone	submarine

Week 15: Activity 1

1. I think Canada is the <u>best</u> country in the world!
2. Which province is the <u>biggest</u>?
3. Jan.
4. Can you get two cookies for me, please?
5. I would also likes a glass of milk.

Week 15: Activity 2

1. Too much ice cream last night.   Not a sentence
2. There are four children in my family.
3. I have one sister and two brothers.
4. mouse : mice
5. bench : benches

Week 15: Activity 3

1. Dawson City 4
2. Max (picked) up the bat, (hit) the ball and (ran) to first base.
3. Gabby (danced) and (sang) in the show and (bowed) at the end.
4. He ate a big piece of chocolate cake.
5. My mom made pancakes for breakfast this morning.

Week 15: Activity 4

1. (The squirrels and chipmunks) are gathering nuts.
2. (Alex and Andy) are running a race.
3. Does your Aunt Wanda live in Saskatoon?
4. She comes to visit your family each July, doesn't she?
5. dice : nice, lice, twice, ice ....

Week 15: Activity 5

Yum! Yum!
...5... Eat and enjoy!
...2... Put the slices of bread into the toaster.
....4.. Sprinkle some brown sugar and cinnamon on the buttered toast.
...3... Butter the toasted bread.
...1... Take out two slices of bread.

Bonus Activity: Canada's Countryside

s	k	c	o	r		b	u	g	s
f	t					i			d
l	g	r	a	s	s	r			o
o		e				d	p		o
w			a			s	o		w
e		s	l	a	m	i	n	a	
r						d			
s	l	l	i	h		s			

Week 16: Activity 1

1. We opened our books and began to read. Classroom, library
2. Mom bought (new) (red) shoes.
3. That (little), (spotted) puppy is named Woof.
4. Why didn't you come over to play last night?
5. We played soccer, basketball, and tag.

Week 16: Activity 2

1. Dinosaurs roamed the province of Alberta.   Real
2. inner : dinner, winner, thinner
3. dash : crash, flash, mash, clash
4. My cousin and I saw an octopus at Marine Marvels.
5. It had eight long arms and squirted blue ink.

WEEK 16: ACTIVITY 3

1. "Let's play Hide and Seek," said Eddie.
2. "Okay.   You're It," replied Paula
3. Wow! What a great bike! Exclamation
4. Did you brush your teeth and comb your hair?
5. The teacher liked my story called The Shy Dragon.

WEEK 16: ACTIVITY 4

1. Does she like to watch a movie with you?
2. Did the baby's toy fall on the floor?
3. Superman   Proper
4. wagons   common
5. wolves : wolf

WEEK 16: ACTIVITY 5

1. Our sun makes its own <u>light.</u>
2. When the sun shines, it gives off <u>heat.</u>
3. This heat keeps us <u>warm.</u>
4. Plants need the sun to help them <u>grow.</u>
5. The sun helps us to grow <u>food.</u>

BONUS ACTIVITY: A NEW PLAYGROUND

Check drawing for accuracy of details requested.

WEEK 17: ACTIVITY 1

1. Do you want to go swimming with us?
2. Don't leave those toys on the stairs.
3. dresses : dress
4. slammed : slam
5. head   spread   ahead

WEEK 17: ACTIVITY 2

1. dentist   James   nurse   .
2. They are coming to our house to visit on Thursday.
3. Did that bear eat some berries from the bush?
4. Peter's marbles
5. The farmer's horse

WEEK 17: ACTIVITY 3

1. The <u>weather</u> is warm today.   Noun
2. Sometimes it <u>rains</u> for days.   Verb
3. camera
4. What would you like for your birthday present?
5. There were a lot of mice in Grandpa's barn.

WEEK 17: ACTIVITY 4

1. Icebergs can be seen in the Atlantic Ocean.   Real
2. Lions roam wild in Alberta.   Make-believe
3. We love to hear the story <u>Charlotte's Web</u> .
4. Fern owns a pig named Wilbur who meets Charlotte.
5. huge : big, giant   small : little, tiny

WEEK 17: ACTIVITY 5

Cause and Effect

1. If you fall into the pond   3 * it will die.
2. If you sleep in   1 * you will get wet.
3. If you don't water the plant   5 * you will get them all right.
4. If you join our game   2 * you might be late for school.
5. If you study your spelling words   4 * you will have fun.

BONUS ACTIVITY: ARCTIC ANIMALS

1. seal
2. wolf
3. caribou
4. polar bear
5. Arctic fox

WEEK 18: ACTIVITY 1

1. Dad has <u>taken</u> our car to the garage.
2. My sister will be skating in the Ice Show.
3. The Browns are moving to Winnipeg.
4. I will miss my friends, Brandon and Kent.
5. At our winter carnival, we made (snowmen), a (snowfort) and giant (snowballs.)

WEEK 18: ACTIVITY 2

1. It was raining <u>cats and dogs.</u>   Very hard, lots of rain
2. He was walking along <u>like a snail.</u>   Very slowly
3. "Will you feed the dog?" asked Mom.
4. "Don't forget to give it water," she added.
5. The day of the party arrived at last. Sentence

SSR1145   ISBN: 9781771587310 © On The Mark Press

WEEK 18: ACTIVITY 3

1. Katie said, "Those girls like to ride horses."
2. "Which girl races and jumps?" I asked.
3. Montreal   3
4. Sudbury   3
5. bee   three   sea   key

WEEK 18: ACTIVITY 4

1. ..4... hand   ...1.. habit   ..3... hall   ..5...
   hard   ..2... hair
2. Mother robin pulled a long worm from the ground.
3. She flew to her nest to feed her babies.
4. "Would you like a menu?" asked the
   waitress.   Restaurant
5. "On your mark.   Get set. Go!"   At a race,
   track meet

WEEK 18: ACTIVITY 5

1. I am going to the zoo.
2. Parkwood Zoo is very large.
3. There are many wild animals to see.
4. The hippos and the giraffes are next to each other.
5. I am going to work at a zoo some day.

BONUS ACTIVITY: ADVERBS

1. My brother and I plant seeds (indoors) in March.
2. The plants grow (slowly) at first.
3. (Later), we plant the tiny plants (outdoors.)
4. The warm sun makes them grow (quickly.)
5. (Soon) there are plants (everywhere!)

WEEK 19: ACTIVITY 1

1. Garth says he wants a hamster for a pet.
2. He thinks they are fumy, little animals.
3. We need to pack our swimsuits, towels and some
   lunch.   Going to the beach
4. tall : short
5. cloudy : sunny

WEEK 19: ACTIVITY 2

1. draw   cause   raw   auto
2. Mom says vegetables are good for you to eat.
3. I like corn, carrots, peas, and potatoes.
4. nickle   dime   quarter
5. oranges   apples   peaches

WEEK 19: ACTIVITY 3

1. furry   strong   hunts
2. The sun (shone on the water.)
3. The mother (sang a song to her baby.)
4. Will you come to my house to play on Saturday?
5. Let's build a play farm with animals and barns.

WEEK 19: ACTIVITY 4

1. "Remember, practice is after school
   tonight."   The coach of your team
2. "This glass slipper fits just right."   Cinderella or
   the Prince
3. isn't
4. Which story do you like the best, Gone or Happy
   Harry ?
5. I like Gone because it is a mystery story.

WEEK 19: ACTIVITY 5

1. (c)arter has to go to the dentist on (t)uesday.
2. (h)is dentist, (d)r. (a)shton, is very nice.
3. (h)er office is on (b)ank (s)treet in (o)ttawa.
4. (c)arter is going with his (a)unt (c)arrie.
5. (m)aybe they will go to (p)izza (h)ut for lunch.

BONUS ACTIVITY   ON THE FARM I HEAR .....

Check speech bubbles for accuracy of sound / animal
match.

WEEK 20: ACTIVITY 1

1. Bee is to hive as bird is to nest
2. cupcake : cup   cake
3. lighthouse : light   house
4. Will you help me with this homework?
5. Miss Melrose said we need to finish it for Friday.

WEEK 20: ACTIVITY 2

1. We are going go skating at the Woodstock Arena.
2. Let's meet there at 7:00 on Thursday night.
3. toboggan 3
4. snowshoe 2
5. hockey team   Answers will vary.

WEEK 20: ACTIVITY 3

1. Thurs.
2. My baby sister, Amy, cries when she is hungry.
3. My mom feeds her and rocks her to sleep.
4. won't : will not
5. they'll : they will / shall

WEEK 20: ACTIVITY 4

1. careless : care
2. untie : tie
3. Mr. and Mrs. Lee are going away to Halifax.
4. They are leaving at 8:00 on Friday morning.
5. hammer   nails   saw

WEEK 20: ACTIVITY 5

1. Carols hair is curly but Annas hair is straight.
   Carol's   Anna's
2. That girls dress is very fancy.   girl's
3. Jacobs wagon has a broken wheel.   Jacob's
4. Dannys new winter coat is red and
   black.   Danny's
5. My brothers dream is to be a baseball
   player.   brother's

BONUS ACTIVITY: YOU, THE ARTIST

Check illustrations for accuracy of details.

WEEK 21: ACTIVITY 1

1. Where are we going for lunch   Question
2. Today is Eddie's birthday   Statement
3. Gayle is the shortest girl in our whole class.
4. My toys are all in that blue box.
5. happiness: happy

WEEK 21: ACTIVITY 2

1. Mr. Larson is our next door neighbour.
2. He works with my dad in Cranbrook.
3. dark : bark, lark, mark, spark
4. came : lame, name, same, flame, blame
5. When the bell ran, we went to our bus.   School

WEEK 21: ACTIVITY 3

1. letter   cupcake   pizza
2. Dad's new car has a flat tire.
3. He will have to get it fixed soon.
4. Every time it snows, we don't go to
   school.   Make-believe
5. If there is an ice storm, roads are very
   slippery.   Real

WEEK 21: ACTIVITY 4

1. Cats, rabbits, and hamsters have very soft fur.
2. They can be many different colours too.
3. germ : j
4. glow : g
5. men

WEEK 21: ACTIVITY 5

1. a school of fish
2. a team of soccer players
3. a fleet of ships
4. a flock of birds
5. a herd of cows

BONUS ACTIVITY: GOODIE FOODIE

selppa	sechee	leryec	rotracs	warsierebrst
apples	cheese	celery	carrots	strawberries

WEEK 22: ACTIVITY 1

1. outdoors : out doors
2. clubhouse : clubhouse
3. include
4. Look out for that big puddle!
5. My pet kitten is black and white.

WEEK 22: ACTIVITY 2

1. wonderful :3
2. Popcorn is my favourite treat.   It
3. My sister and I get it every time we go to a
   movie.   We
4. I went to the park with Janie, Sally and Marie.
5. We played tag for two hours.

SSR1145   ISBN: 9781771587310 © On The Mark Press

WEEK 22: ACTIVITY 3

1. Fur is to cat as feathers are to bird.
2. Pumpkin is to vine as apple is to tree.
3. beaver   raccoon   chipmunk
4. We are getting ready for the Terry Fox Run.
5. It is going to be on Sunday, September 17, 2017.

WEEK 22: ACTIVITY 4

1. She cleans and fixes our teeth.   Dentist
2. Gerry asked me to his birthday party.
3. We are going to go bowling and to Sam's Snacks for treats.
4. You need to wash your hands.   They are <u>filthy.</u>   Very dirty
5. We <u>probably</u> will go to the movie tonight.   Likely

WEEK 22: ACTIVITY 5

1. Patti, Wendy, and I are going to the beach.
2. We are taking sandwiches, drinks, and cupcakes to eat.
3. We need shovels, pails, and pretty stones to build a sand castle.
4. We were proud of our castle.   It looked great!
5. Do you like to build sand castles?   We do!

BONUS ACTIVITY: JUST LIKE THE ANIMALS

	My picture
1. as quiet as a mouse	
2. swims like a fish	
3. stubborn as a mule	
4. hungry as a bear	

WEEK 23: ACTIVITY 1

1. "I'm hungry. I need a snack," said Lila.
2. "Why don't you have an apple?" I replied.
3. This fairy tale tells about an <u>ogre.</u>   Monster, imaginary creature
4. That is <u>Colin's</u> hockey stick.
5. <u>Fanny's</u> mom is a doctor.

WEEK 23: ACTIVITY 2

1. Did Mr. Murray's dog have seven puppies?
2. What's he going to do with so many puppies?
3. We sat under the (tree) to eat our (lunch.)
4. My (sister) brought her (doll) to (school.)
5. they are : they're

WEEK 23: ACTIVITY 3

1. Jackson is on the same team as Willy, Ted, and Seth.
2. They played a good game last Saturday in Danville Park.
3. harder   softer
4. Fruits are good for us.   Real
5. Bananas grow in Ontario.   Make-believe

WEEK 23: ACTIVITY 4

1. Dear Aunt Susie,
2. baby :babies
3. fox : foxes
4. Who won the Public Speaking contest?
5. I think it was that new girl, Lynne.

WEEK 23: ACTIVITY 5

1. Last week, a police officer <u>visited</u> our classroom.
2. I <u>like</u> it when a guest comes to our school.
3. She <u>talked</u> about how we can keep safe.
4. Ms Harris <u>thanked</u> the officer for coming.
5. I <u>hope</u> we have another visitor soon.

BONUS ACTIVITY   WEATHER WORDS

frost	rock	sleet	train	lightning
snow	tree	cloudy	sled	fog
rain	sunny	thunder	birds	flurries
storm	flower	blizzard	bees	drizzle
windy	car	hail	shark	mist

WEEK 24: ACTIVITY 1

1. Joey began to cry <u>when he broke his new toy truck.</u>
2. Did she give those cookies to her friend Ruby.
3. Mrs. Adams rode the bus home from work.
4. bear is to growl as dog is to bark
5. blue is to sky as green is to grass

Week 24: Activity 2

1. geese
2. mice .
3. Dr. Barton lives in a big house in the country.
4. He is a vet who looks after farm animals.
5. Clean up that mess before you go
   outside.   Command

Week 24: Activity 3

1. I saw an elf playing in the garden.   Make-
   believe
2. Do you like ketchup and mustard on your hot
   dogs?
3. I think Karl broke his glasses.
4. My brother and I are staying home tonight.   We
5. Mom and Dad are going out for dinner.   They

Week 24: Activity 4

1. How did Marc lose his hat and mittens?
2. Mike, Guy and Larry fed peanuts to those squirrels.
3. street : St.
4. September : Sept.
5. The stars are shining brightly tonight.   Noun

Week 24: Activity 5   What Happens Next?

1. The telephone began to ring.
   (b) I will answer it.
2. Jay dropped the glass and broke it.
   (a) He will tell his mom.
3. Mother Hen sat on the eggs for days.
   (b) The chicks hatched.
4. After the rain, the sun was shining.
   (a) We saw a rainbow.
5. I got a great book at the library.
   (b) I will start to read it.

Bonus Activity: Great Covers!

Camping Adventures	Cooking for Kids	Canadian Trees
	1. This book has ideas for foods kids can cook.	1. This book tells facts about Canada's trees.
2. This book tells how to have fun camping.		

Week 25: Activity 1

1. Addie and I can't go to the Hallowe'en party.
2. I don't like turnip, beets, or carrots
3. That (small) (brown) button fell off his coat.
4. We rolled (big) snowballs to make that (giant) snowfort.
5. What are they going to do on Saturday?

Week 25: Activity 2

1. She has gone shopping with her Aunt Libby.
2. I think they have gone to the Yorkdale Mall.
3. Hurray Our team won   Exclamation
4. New Brunswick : 3
5. Saskatchewan : 4

Week 25: Activity 3

1. CN Tower   proper noun
2. railroad common noun
3. Edna found four Easter eggs under her bed.
4. How did Bernie get all those right answers?.
5. _1_ eagle   _3_ egg   _2_ eel   _5_ empty   _4_ elk

SSR1145   ISBN: 9781771587310 © On The Mark Press

WEEK 25: ACTIVITY 4

1. Give me a cookie and a glass of milk.
2. We began to wash the dishes after dinner.
3. huge   large
4. The best sport   Not a sentence
5. I love poutine!   Sentence

WEEK 25: ACTIVITY 5

Dear Grandpa,

May I come to your house this weekend? Maybe we could go fishing. I would love fish for supper!

Love,
Brad

BONUS ACTIVITY: HOMOPHONES

Picture of hair	ball	sun	whale	Student picture
hair	ball	sun	whale	pair pear

WEEK 26: ACTIVITY 1

1. I had fun playing at Jake's house last Saturday.   Past
2. Let's set the table for dinner.   Present
3. Those boys were running and jumping and laughing.
4. Hank dug a hole to plant his little tree.
5. 7 is to number as M is to letter.

WEEK 26: ACTIVITY 2

1. start, begin   Same
2. prince, princess   Opposite
3. mountain goat : 3
4. Mrs. Carter told us a funny story about a baby bear.
5. This bear liked to pick berries to eat.

WEEK 26: ACTIVITY 3

1. Jack and Jill went up the hill.   They
2. The pail of water tumbled down the hill.   It
3. Our class is going to go up in the CN Tower.
4. Will you be afraid to go to the top?
5. The player hit a home run.   Baseball game

WEEK 26: ACTIVITY 4

1. When can he and I play that game?
2. Does a spider have eight legs?
3. John is going to the dentist tomorrow.
4. She will sing at the concert on Sunday.
5. bee   wasp   ant

WEEK 26: ACTIVITY 5   COMBINING SENTENCES

1. Grandma baked cookies and muffins.
2. My aunt loves books and movies.
3. The dog barked and wagged its tail.
4. Dad started the lawnmower to cut the grass.
5. Donnie told a funny joke so we laughed.

BONUS ACTIVITY: SH! SILENT LETTERS

Clue					
1. A dog does this to a bone.	g	n	a	w	*	*
2. We use this for our hair.	c	o	m	b	*	*
3. You can tie this in a rope.	k	n	o	t	*	*
4. We use this to cut things.	k	n	i	f	e	*
5. We do this on a door.	k	n	o	c	k	*
6. I can fight battles and dragons.	k	n	i	g	h	t

WEEK 27: ACTIVITY 1

1. Have you ever read The Night Before Christmas ?
2. He doesn't have any money left in his piggy bank.
3. she'll : she will / shall
4. that's : that is
5. joyful   happy

WEEK 27: ACTIVITY 2

1. foot : feet
2. child : children
3. Jules dropped the glass and broke it.
4. Paige wants to play with Bella and Josie.
5. They are making up a play about a magical horse.

WEEK 27: ACTIVITY 3

1. It is safe to swim in the <u>shallow</u> end of the pool.   Not deep
2. Mosquitoes were a <u>nuisance</u> to us on our hike.   Pest
3. Do you want to go to summer camp?
4. I go to Camp Wellwood every summer in July.
5. clean

WEEK 27: ACTIVITY 4

1. glow: blow, flow, snow, mow, grows.
2. A mouse ran fast across our floor.
3. Then it ran under my bed and hid.
4. The world's largest (bird) is an (ostrich).
5. (Gina) can play the (piano) and the (harp).

WEEK 27: ACTIVITY 5

1. Jacko is the smartest parrot in the pet shop.
2. Bill is tall but his brother is taller.
3. Maggy loves chocolate ice cream the best.
4. David runs quicker than I run.
5. The Smith children live near the school.

BONUS ACTIVITY: GROWING IN CANADA, YOU WILL FIND ....

w			m	a	p	l	e	s	
	i		e			l		p	
		l			p			r	
	m		l	p		i		u	
		k		a	o		n	c	
				a	w			e	
				s					
b	i	r	c	h	r	a	d	e	c

WEEK 28: ACTIVITY 1

1. David's football
2. the girls' bicycles
3. Are you going to come shopping with us?
4. We are gonna go early on Saturday morning.
5. Timmy went camping last weekend at Sand Lake.   Past

WEEK 28: ACTIVITY 2

1. Get your ticket and line up for the ride.   Carnival, fair
2. Aunt Kami's present arrived on May 21, 2012.
3. How many children were at your party?
4. Robins make their nests in trees.   Real
5. Cats that are pets will not chase birds.   Make-believe

WEEK 28: ACTIVITY 3

1. Did dinosaurs ever live in Alberta   Question
2. Scientists have found many bones there   Statement
3. gum   going   gate.
4. Why weren't you eating those cookies?
5. My friends, Les and Luke, are twins.

WEEK 28: ACTIVITY 4

1. cow is to moo as cat is to meow
2. He and I went biking to that park.
3. What's the best game to play indoors?
4. She screamed (loudly) when she saw the bug.
5. The fish flopped (wildly) on the hook.

WEEK 28: ACTIVITY 5

1. I have a secret to tell you.   S
2. Do you promise not to tell anyone?   Q
3. Tomorrow is my birthday.   S
4. Hooray, it's finally here!   E
5. Come to my house on Saturday to my party.   C

BONUS ACTIVITY: SNOW DAY!

...5...   They made a big snowman in their backyard.
...2...   In the morning, Max looked out the window.
....4..   Max and his sister went outside to play.
...1...   It snowed and snowed all night.
...3...   "School buses are cancelled today," said Mom.

WEEK 29: ACTIVITY 1

1. Can you tell Aunt Beth I will visit on Sunday?
2. If you climb that tree, don't fall.
3. teeth : more than one
4. helmet : one
5. Study your words for your spelling test.   Command

SSR1145   ISBN: 9781771587310 © On The Mark Press

Week 29: Activity 2

1. Did she remember to take her two books to school?
2. I want to read the poem <u>Alligator Pie.</u>
3. We all <u>clapped</u> for the singer,
4. Dad is <u>running</u> in the big race.
5. Mary's

Week 29: Activity 3

1. Who is going to be your new teacher?
2. I think it well be Mr. Gordon.
3. Nova Scotia   Proper noun
4. tides   Common noun
5. Spud is a (brown) and (white) bulldog.

Week 29: Activity 4

1. closest : close
2. skipping : skip
3. Give me a glass of cold water, please.
4. Those cats are good at catching mice.
5. Vancouver Island : 5

Week 29: Activity 5   Homophones

1. I <u>sent</u> out invitations to my birthday party.
2. I was allowed to invite <u>four</u> friends.
3. If it doesn't <u>rain,</u> we are going on a hike.
4. We will go by an old cabin made of <u>wood.</u>
5. Last week, Dad and I saw two deer near the cabin.

Bonus Activity: I Love the Beach

swimsuit (Y)	dig (B)	play (B)	swim (B)
hat (Y)	beach towel (Y)	shovel (Y)	run (B)
sandwiches (Y)	build (B)	snacks (Y)	sunglasses (Y)

Week 30: Activity 1

1. A beaver's home is called a lodge.   Real
2. When are you coming to see me?
3. We can have a sleep-over in my tent.
4. apples
5. circle

Week 30: Activity 2

1. cry, laugh   Opposite
2. "Were there ants on the picnic table?" asked Cam.
3. "No, I scared them all away," said Maggy.
4. colourful : 3
5. Summerside : 3

Week 30: Activity 3

1. He just learned to ride his new bike.
2. Who is going help me make my bed?
3. queen   .
4. our
5. what

Week 30: Activity 4

1. We liked the story <u>The Littlest Dragon.</u>
2. Ms Dawson read it to us last week.
3. happy   merry   glad
4. will not : won't
5. is not : isn't

Week 30: Activity 5

1. Kelly gave <u>Kim</u> some of her popcorn.   her
2. I ride on <u>a bus</u> to school.   it
3. We cheered for <u>Ronnie and David</u> to win the race.   them
4. Mrs. Hartley gave <u>my class</u> a treat.   us
5. Did you see <u>the rainbow</u> yesterday?   it

Bonus Activity: Make New Words

1. Change <u>notes</u> into a small rock.   stone
2. Change <u>lump</u> into a sweet, purple fruit.   plum
3. Change <u>shore</u> into an animal a cowboy rides.   horse
4. Change <u>swap</u> into an insect that will sting you.   wasp
5. Change <u>stool</u> into things we use to work.   tools

Week 31: Activity 1

1. That (red) van belongs to our (new) neighbour.
2. I love (chocolate) cake with (white) icing!
3. Bears eat lots of food in the spring and summer.
4. Then they go to sleep for the whole winter.
5. Betty screamed when a mouse ran across the floor.

Week 31: Activity 2

1. buttercup : butter cup
2. basketball : basket ball
3. My friend, Bruce, and I like to do the same things.
4. Sometimes we play baseball, football, or golf.
5. We ran inside when it started to rain.

Week 31: Activity 3

1. cars
2. squirrels
3. grandfather : 3
4. Little Miss Muffet sat on her tuffet to eat.
5. A big, black, hairy spider scared her away.

Week 31: Activity 4

1. (Yesterday) I ran home (quickly).
2. His pet rabbit is named Boomer.
3. Isn't that a funny name for a pet rabbit?
4. Stand right here   Sentence
5. All alone   Not a sentence

Week 31: Activity 5

1. Dale, Matt, Hal, and Nate are playing a game.
2. It snowed on Saturday, Sunday, Monday, and Tuesday.
3. My family likes to skate, toboggan, ski, and sled.
4. Her favourite snacks are cookies, apples, carrots, and chips.
5. In school, we study math, science, reading, and music.

Bonus Activity

My title is _____

I have a pet hamster named Patches.	He likes to hide in the wood shavings.	He likes to stuff his cheeks with food.	At night, he runs and runs on his wheel.

Check to see if details in the illustration match the sentences.

Week 32: Activity 1

1. What did that man ask you?
2. Did those girls go swimming in the lake?
3. stood   hood
4. start   begin   Same
5. quick   slow   Opposite

Week 32: Activity 2

1. The tulips started to bloom.   Spring
2. When I grow up, I'm going to be a doctor.
3. The carpenter built a fence out of boards.
4. All cats have whiskers.
5. Jessie hates dill pickles.

Week 32: Activity 3

1. The oldest boy.   Not a sentence
2. My mother called me.   Sentence
3. Grandpa eat eggs, bacon, and toast for breakfast.
4. Clean up that mess right now.
5. duck is to duckling as hen is to chick

Week 32: Activity 4

1. peaches
2. Let's plant beans, carrot,s and corn in our garden.
3. Alec and John are twins who live next door.
4. sheep : deep, keep, leap, peep
5. goat : boat, coat, moat, float

Week 32: Activity 5

October 1, 2017.

Dear Joan,

Would you like to come to my house for Thanksgiving dinner? My mom is cooking a big turkey. She also will cook potatoes, gravy, carrots, and corn. We have pumpkin pie for dessert.

Your friend,

Patti

Bonus Activity: A Not – So – Secret Message!

C	a	n	a	d	a		i	s		m	y		h	o	m	e		!
d	b	o	b	e	b		j	t		n	z		i	p	n	f		!

SSR1145   ISBN: 9781771587310 © On The Mark Press